SINGER

SEWING REFERENCE LIBRARY®

Quick & Easy
Sewing Projects

Cy DeCosse Incorporated
Minnetonka, Minnesota

SINGER

SEWING REFERENCE LIBRARY®

Quick & Easy
Sewing Projects

Contents

QUICK & EASY SEWING PROJECTS
Created by: The Editors of Cy DeCosse
  Incorporated, in cooperation with
  the Sewing Education Department,
  Singer Sewing Company. Singer is a
  trademark of The Singer Company and
  is used under license.

Library of Congress
Cataloging-in-Publication Data

Quick & easy sewing projects.

p. cm. — (Singer sewing reference
library)
Includes index.
ISBN 0-86573-288-4
ISBN 0-86573-289-2 (pbk.)
1. Machine sewing. 2. Clothing and dress.
3. House furnishings. I. Cy DeCosse
Incorporated. II. Title: Quick and easy
sewing projects. III. Series.
TT713.Q53 1993
646.2 — dc20   93-25891

CY DECOSSE INCORPORATED
Chairman: Cy DeCosse
President: James B. Maus
Executive Vice President: William B. Jones

Also available from the publisher:
*Sewing Essentials, Sewing for the Home, Clothing
Care & Repairs, Sewing for Style, Sewing Specialty
Fabrics, Sewing Activewear, The Perfect Fit,
Timesaving Sewing, More Sewing for the Home,
Sewing Update, Tailoring, Sewing for Children,
Sewing with an Overlock, 101 Sewing Secrets,
Sewing Pants That Fit, Quilting by Machine,
Decorative Machine Stitching, Creative Sewing
Ideas, Sewing Lingerie, Sewing Projects for the
Home, Sewing with Knits, More Creative Sewing
Ideas, Quilt Projects by Machine, Creating Fashion
Accessories, Sewing for Special Occasions, Sewing
for the Holidays*

Executive Editor: Zoe A. Graul
Senior Technical Director: Rita C. Opseth
Senior Project Manager: Joseph Cella
Project Manager: Diane Dreon-Krattiger
Art Director: Mark Jacobson
Senior Art Director: Delores Swanson
Writer: Rita C. Opseth
Editor: Janice Cauley
Research Assistant: Linda Neubauer
Sample Coordinator: Carol Olson
Styling Director: Bobbette Destiche
Senior Technical Photo Stylist: Bridget
  Haugh
Fabric Editor: Joanne Wawra
Assistant Fabric Editor: Marie Castle
Sewing Staff: Sharon Eklund, Corliss
  Forstrom, Phyllis Galbraith, Sara
  Macdonald, Linda Neubauer, Carol
  Pilot, Nancy Sundeen

*Vice President of Development Planning
  & Production:* Jim Bindas
Production Manager: Amelia Merz
Studio Manager: Mike Parker
Assistant Studio Managers: Marcia
  Chambers, Rena Tassone
Creative Photo Coordinator: Cathleen
  Shannon
Lead Photographer: Paul Najlis
Photographers: Rebecca Hawthorne, Rex
  Irmen, John Lauenstein, Billy
  Lindner, Mark Macemon, Chuck
  Nields, Mike Parker
Contributing Photographers: Kim Bailey,
  Doug Deutscher, Paul Markert
Photo Stylist: Susan Pasqual
Electronic Publishing Specialist: Joe Fahey
Production Staff: Stephanie Beck, Adam
  Esco, Mike Hehner, Jim Huntley, Phil
  Juntti, Janet Morgan, Robert Powers,

  Mike Schauer, Linda Schloegel, Greg
  Wallace, Kay Wethern, Nik Wogstad
Consultants: Wendy Fedie, Corliss
  Forstrom, Pamela Hastings, Jeanne
  Johnson, Judy Laube, Marlys
  Riedesel, Sue Stein, Ruth Stephens
Contributors: Coats & Clark Inc.;
  Creative Beginnings; Dyno
  Merchandise Corporation; EZ
  International; Fairfield Processing
  Corporation; HTC-Handler Textile
  Corporation; Olfa® Products
  International; Spartex Inc.; Streamline
  Industries, Inc.; Swiss-Metrosene, Inc.
Printed on American paper by:
Arcata Graphics Company (1094)

Introduction

Sewing can be fun, fast, and easy. Beginners and advanced sewers alike enjoy the instant reward of no-hassle sewing projects. This book is filled with clothes, accessories, children's toys, and home decorating projects that are quick and easy.

The Easy Clothes section of the book will help you sew a new wardrobe. Save time by making a jacket from a blanket, to eliminate the need for facings and interfacings and to utilize simple collar and closure techniques. Add the detailing of pieced inserts to a basic purchased shirt, and enjoy the creative part of sewing without all the work of sewing a collar, plackets, and cuffs. Then add your own creative accents to plain T-shirts. Make a slim skirt from two-way stretch fabric for a stylish garment with quick fitting, and use the microwave oven to crinkle-pleat a long, full skirt that is fast to make and carefree to wear.

The Easy Clothes section also includes garments for children. Make rompers for infants and toddlers from button-front shirts of flannels and shirtings, or from T-shirts. Or sew a child's puppy bath poncho from terry towels.

In the Quick Accessories section, learn how to make creative envelope purses and embellish them with decorative painting and studs. Or for a roomier bag, sew the drawstring duffle. Make outdoor accessories that will keep you and your family warm, using fleece for quick construction without seam finishes. No patterns are required for the mittens, scarves, headbands, neckwarmers, and booties.

The Fun Toys to Sew section features toys for all ages. Make your own kites from lightweight nylon and wooden dowels, choosing either the fringed delta or the arch-top kite. Both are easy to construct and fly easily too. Sew a small teddy bear, or the ladybug and spider hand puppets, using the pattern pieces included. This section even shows you how to make a playhouse tent that can be used indoors and out.

Home Decorating Projects includes several styles of placemats, pillows, and lamp shade covers. And for outside the home, we have even included a wind sock. Whatever you like to sew--clothes, accessories, toys, or home decorating projects--you will find lots of ideas in this book. From cover to cover, this book has step-by-step instructions for dozens of quick and easy projects.

Quick Accessories (opposite), pages 48 to 69.

Home Decorating Projects (right), pages 98 to 125.

Easy Clothes, pages 8 to 47.

Fun Toys to Sew, pages 70 to 97.

Easy Clothes

Fringed Jackets
from Blankets

This lightweight jacket is made from a reversible cotton throw blanket. Blankets, fringed on all four sides, are available in a wide variety of designs and colors. The size varies from one blanket to another; select one that measures about 50" × 60" (127 × 152.5 cm). Only one blanket is needed if you follow the cutting layout below. However, two blankets may be needed if you change the layout to take advantage of certain design details in the blanket or if a small blanket size is used.

Select a commercial pattern for a single-breasted cardigan jacket with a low V neck and dropped shoulders. The pattern should have relatively straight side seams and no darts. Only the jacket front, jacket back, and sleeve pattern pieces will be used; the collar pattern is created during construction.

The full width of the blanket is used for the jacket so that the front and lower edges are fringed. Depending on the size of the blanket, the jacket may or may not overlap in the front. Either way, this fringed jacket, with its relaxed fit, looks equally attractive. For decorative purposes, add conchos and leather ties to the jacket front.

✂ Cutting Directions

Prepare the pattern as on page 12, steps 1 and 2. Lay out and cut the jacket body and sleeves as in steps 3 and 4, reserving a strip along one fringed edge of the blanket, measuring at least 6" × 40" (15 × 102 cm), for the collar. Prepare the shawl collar pattern and cut the collar along the fringed edge of the blanket as in steps 7 to 9. (See the cutting layout below.)

YOU WILL NEED

One or two woven cotton throw blankets, about 50" × 60" (127 × 152.5 cm).

Commercial pattern for single-breasted V-necked cardigan jacket with dropped shoulders.

Two conchos.

1¼ yd. (115 m) leather lacing.

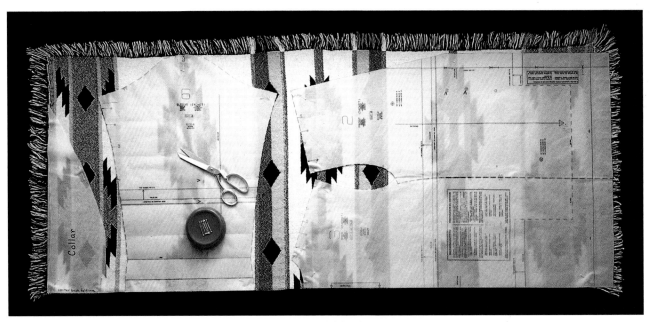

Cutting layout for the jacket body and sleeves on a fringed blanket.

How to Sew a Fringed Jacket from a Blanket

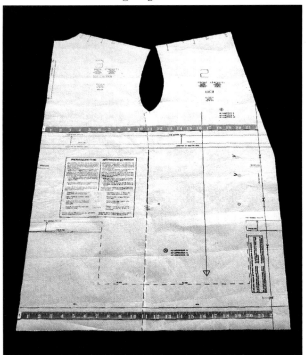

1) Tape the jacket front pattern piece to jacket back pattern piece at side seams, aligning the seamlines at the armhole and overlapping seam allowances at sides. Keep center back parallel to center front.

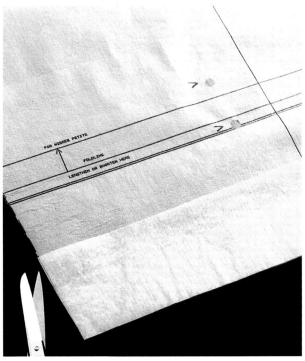

2) Extend the sleeve hem allowance to 4" (10 cm), to allow for a turned-back cuff with a narrow hem. At hemline, fold pattern and trace cutting line for hem allowance, following cutting line of sleeve.

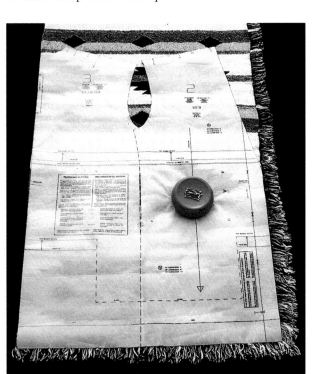

3) Fold the blanket in half lengthwise, matching any horizontal designs. Pin the jacket body pattern to blanket, with center back of pattern on lengthwise fold of blanket and hemline of pattern on inner edge of fringe. The center front will be at or near fringe.

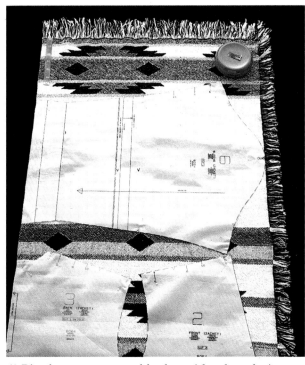

4) Pin sleeve pattern to blanket, either lengthwise or crosswise, depending on the desired placement of the blanket design. For the collar, reserve an area about 6" × 40" (15 × 102 cm) along fringed edge. Use a second blanket, if necessary.

5) Cut jacket body and sleeves. Pin and stitch the shoulder seams, right sides together; finish seams, using overlock or zigzag stitch. Press seams toward jacket back. Topstitch through all layers.

6) Measure raw edge at neckline from center back to the inner edge of fringe on front of jacket; stand the tape measure on edge for accurate measuring.

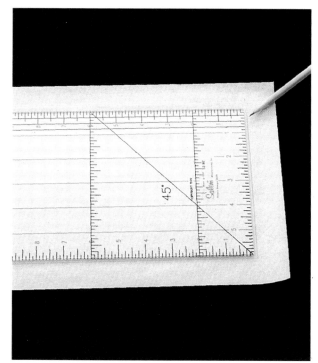

7) Make collar pattern on tissue paper, drawing a long straight line to be placed on the inner edge of blanket fringe; draw 6" (15 cm) perpendicular line, for center back foldline.

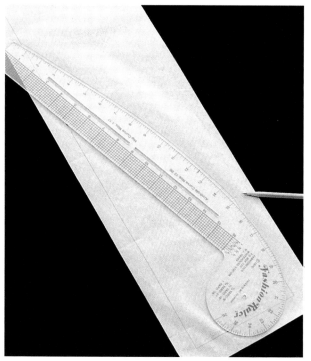

8) Draw 6" (15 cm) line, parallel to long straight line, beginning at the end of center back foldline. Using a curved ruler, draw a line that curves from end of this line to long straight line; total length of line, including the 6" (15 cm) portion, should be 2" (5 cm) longer than measurement in step 6.

(Continued on next page)

9) Pin collar pattern to blanket, with the center back foldline on fold of blanket and long straight edge of pattern along inner edge of blanket fringe. Cut out the collar.

10) Pin raw edge of collar to jacket, with right side of collar on wrong side of jacket, matching center backs. Pin collar, from fringe at front edges to the shoulder seams. Easing in fullness, pin collar to back neckline.

11) Stitch and finish collar seam; press seam toward body of jacket. Topstitch through all layers.

12) Fold the shawl collar back, covering the seam.

13) **Stitch** and finish sleeve seams. Press seams toward back. Press under ½" (1.3 cm) twice on lower edges of sleeves, for double-fold hems; stitch close to fold.

14) **Pin** and stitch sleeves to armholes; finish seams. Press seams toward body of jacket. Topstitch through all layers.

15) **Position** concho at bottom of collar. Separating yarns in weave of jacket with awl, thread the ends of 24" (61 cm) length of leather lacing down, then up, through slots in concho, and through all jacket layers.

16) **Thread** ends of lacing through loop, pulling them tight to form a larkspur knot. Knot ends of lacing.

Purchased Shirts with Pieced Inserts

Create an intricately pieced shirt quickly and easily, starting with a purchased shirt. On each side of the shirt front and back, a section is cut away and replaced with a section of pieced fabrics. The design change does not alter the original size of the shirt.

When adding the inserts, ignore any garment details such as pockets. The unexpected effect of cutting away the pocket to allow for the pieced insert adds character to the garment.

Oversized shirts work well for this project and make a stylish fashion statement. You may even want to use a man's shirt, with rolled-up sleeves. Shoulder pads can be hand-stitched in place to add shape to the shirt.

To dress up a cotton shirt, add pieced inserts of lightweight silky fabrics. For a subtle effect, choose silkies of the same color as the shirt, varying the shades or the textures of the pieces. For a more dramatic look, use silkies that are in strong contrast to the shirt color. Shirtings may be used for the pieced

inserts in a more casual garment; different looks can be created by using solid colors, madras plaids, printed fabrics, or a combination.

Assorted buttons can be stitched onto the placket, spaced between the original buttons of the shirt, for added detailing. Choose pearl buttons or buttons with gold filigree for a dressy look; choose brightly colored shirt buttons for a sporty look.

✂ Cutting Directions

Cut several coordinating fabrics into strips of 2" and 3" (5 and 7.5 cm) widths. Cut each strip into rectangles of various lengths, from 2" to 10" (5 to 25.5 cm).

YOU WILL NEED

Purchased shirt, such as an oversized man's shirt.
Scraps of several fabrics, for pieced inserts.
Small decorative shirt buttons, optional.
Shoulder pads, optional.

How to Add a Pieced Insert to a Shirt

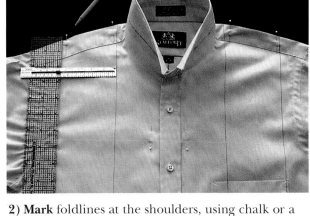

1) Place buttoned shirt on flat surface, folded at side seams, with front of shirt facing up; smooth the shirt from side seams to center; pin as necessary. If shirt has center back pleat, excess fullness will be under the placket.

2) Mark foldlines at the shoulders, using chalk or a water-soluble marking pen. Draw lines 3½" (9 cm) apart, centered on foldlines and parallel to center front; extend lines from shoulders to the lower edge of the shirt.

3) Cut through both the front and the back of the shirt on marked lines, using rotary cutter. Or pin along marked lines so layers will not shift, and cut with shears. Set aside cut sections.

4) Sew 2" (5 cm) pieces together randomly, stitching ¼" (6 mm) seams, to make two 2" (5 cm) pieced strips about 3" (7.5 cm) longer than sections cut from shirt. Finish seams, using zigzag or overlock stitch.

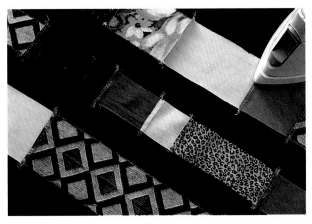

5) Repeat step 4 with 3" (7.5 cm) pieces, to make two 3" (7.5 cm) pieced strips. Press seam allowances of pieced strips in same direction.

6) Place one 2" (5 cm) strip and one 3" (7.5 cm) strip right sides together, matching raw edges; stitch ¼" (6 mm) seam. Finish seam, and press seam allowances toward 3" (7.5 cm) strip. Repeat to make pieced insert from two remaining strips.

7) Fold one insert in half; fold one section cut from shirt at shoulder. Center shirt section over insert, with highest side of shoulder over 3" (7.5 cm) strip. Make sure insert is longer than shirt front and back; fold insert unevenly if front and back are different lengths.

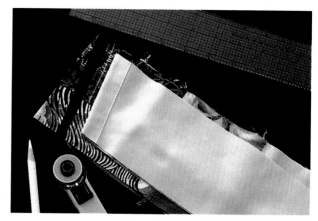

8) Mark the angle of the shoulder on pieced strip. Cut across pieced strip, ¼" (6 mm) beyond marked line.

9) Stitch ¼" (6 mm) shoulder seam in pieced strip. Finish seam; press to one side. Repeat procedure for pieced strip on opposite side of shirt.

10) Pin the pieced strips to shirt, matching placement marks at shoulders of shirt with shoulder seams of strips. Stitch ¼" (6 mm) seams; finish seam. Press seam allowances toward pieced strips.

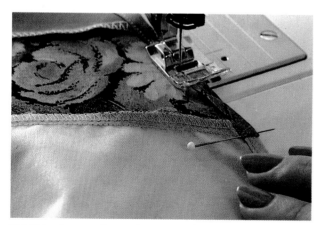

11) Trim lower edges of strips to ½" (6 mm) beyond the original shirt hem. Press and stitch ¼" (6 mm) double-fold hems.

12) Sew additional buttons onto the placket of the shirt, if desired, spacing them between buttonholes. Attach shoulder pads, if desired.

Slim Skirts without a Commercial Pattern

Pull-on knit skirts in two-way stretch fabrics are easy to sew. This slim skirt can be made without using a commercial pattern. The slim style allows only 1" (2.5 cm) of ease at the hipline and tapers slightly at the hem for an attractive fit.

Two-way stretch knits include spandex, an elastic synthetic fiber that gives the fabric excellent stretch and recovery in both the lengthwise and crosswise directions. Two-way stretch knits are available in a variety of colors and textures, suitable for everything from activewear to evening wear. Spandex is often blended with polyester, cotton, or nylon. Prewash two-way stretch fabrics, following the care method recommended by the manufacturer. This preshrinks the fabric and allows fabric that has been wrapped around a bolt to return to its natural shape. Air dry the fabric, because the heat from machine drying can damage the spandex fibers.

Use a narrow zigzag stitch for sewing the seams of the skirt, to provide the necessary stretch. This stitch also allows you to press the seams open so they lie flat, without bulk.

✂ Cutting Directions

Make the pattern, below. Using the pattern, cut one skirt front and one skirt back from two-way stretch fabric, with the center foldline of the pattern along the lengthwise folds of the fabric.

YOU WILL NEED

Fabric with two-way stretch, at least 5" (12.5 cm) wider than hip measurement, yardage equal to desired skirt length plus 5" (12.5 cm).

Elastic, 1" (2.5 cm) wide, length equal to waist measurement.

How to Make a Pattern for a Slim Skirt

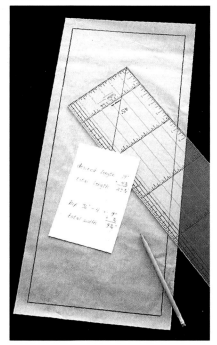 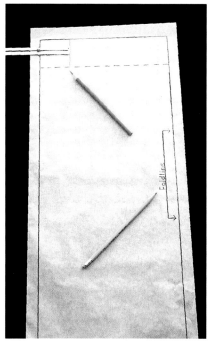 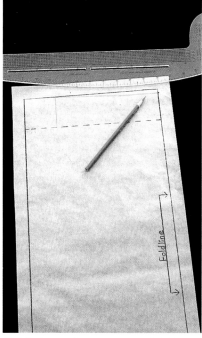

1) Draw rectangle on tracing paper, with length equal to desired skirt length from waistline to lower edge plus 4⅜" (11.2 cm); this allows for hem and casing. Width equals hip measurement divided by four plus ¾" (2 cm); this allows for seam allowances and wearing ease.

2) Mark the approximate waistline 2⅜" (6.2 cm) from the top of the rectangle. Mark center foldline. Draw cutting line from top of the rectangle to waistline, 2¼" (6 cm) from and parallel to side.

3) Mark a point on center foldline, ¼" (6 mm) down from the top of the rectangle. Using curved ruler, draw upper cutting line from this point to cutting line at side.

(Continued on next page)

How to Make a Pattern for a Slim Skirt (continued)

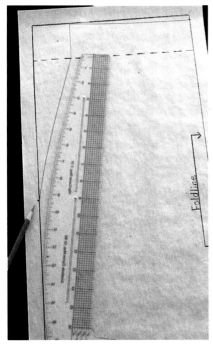

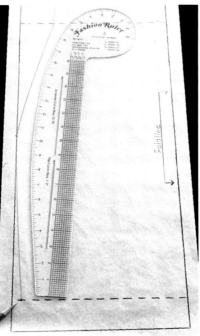

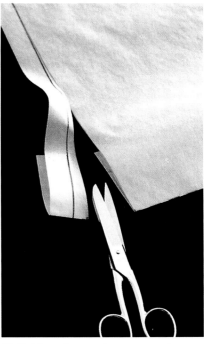

4) Measure your body from waist to fullest part of hips. On side of pattern, measure this distance from waistline; mark. Draw cutting line from the mark for hipline to vertical line at waistline, using a curved ruler.

5) Mark the hemline 1¾" (4.5 cm) from lower edge. Mark a point ½" (1.3 cm) from side of pattern on hemline. Draw cutting line from hemline point to hip point, using a curved ruler.

6) Fold under tracing paper along hemline. Cut out the skirt pattern, cutting through both layers at the hem allowance.

How to Sew a Slim Skirt

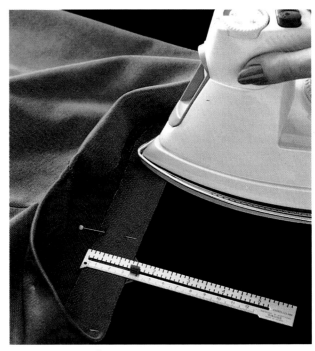

1) Cut skirt front and skirt back as on page 21. Pin front to back, right sides together, matching raw edges at sides. Stitch ½" (1.3 cm) side seams, using short, narrow zigzag stitch; press open.

2) Fold under 1⅜" (3.5 cm) at upper edge of skirt, for casing; pin in place, and press.

3) Stitch casing ¼" (6 mm) from raw edge, using short, narrow zigzag stitch; leave 2" (5 cm) opening in skirt back.

4) Insert elastic in casing; pin ends together, using safety pin. Try on skirt, wrong side out. Adjust elastic so it fits comfortably around waist and pulls easily over hips; repin elastic.

5) Cut elastic, allowing for ½" (1.3 cm) overlap. Lap ends, and stitch securely through both layers, using wide zigzag stitch. Stitch opening of casing closed.

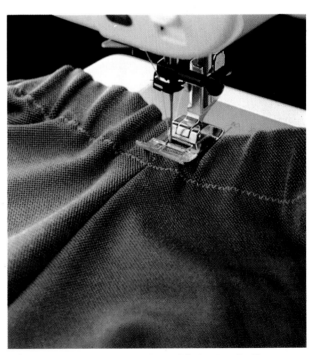

6) Stretch elastic to distribute fabric evenly. From right side of skirt, stitch in the ditch at side seams through all layers, to secure elastic. Fold under 1¾" (4.5 cm) at lower edge; pin and press. Stitch hem.

Microwaved Skirts

A microwave oven is used for setting the crinkles in this unlined, full skirt. For best results, select a sheer or lightweight fabric of 100 percent polyester or a blend of polyester and rayon. A printed georgette, lawn, chiffon, or organza works well.

The skirt is sewn from the fabric before it is crinkled. Then the skirt is soaked in lukewarm water, twisted tightly into a ball, and microwaved. The microwaving process heat-sets the crinkles in the fabric and shortens the drying time. To finish drying the skirt, the twisted ball is then machine dried.

The skirt will keep its shape during wearing. When laundering, maintain the crinkled texture by washing the skirt in cold water and hanging it to dry. For traveling, the skirt can be twisted into a ball and tucked into a corner of a suitcase.

Crinkling the fabric causes it to shrink in both length and width. Cut the skirt lengths 3" (7.5 cm) longer than the desired finished length of the skirt to allow for shrinkage and the necessary seam and hem allowances. Use either three or four widths of fabric for the skirt; if sheer fabric is used, four widths of fabric are recommended. To reduce bulk at the waistline, the skirt has a separate elasticized waistband.

✂ Cutting Directions

Cut three or four skirt sections, 45" (115 cm) wide, with the length of each section 3" (7.5 cm) longer than the desired finished length; for accuracy in cutting on the grainline, pull threads on the crosswise grain. Cut one waistband piece, 4¼" (10.8 cm) wide, with the length of the piece 3" (7.5 cm) longer than your hip measurement.

YOU WILL NEED

Sheer to lightweight fabric of 100 percent polyester or a blend of polyester and rayon.

Elastic, 1½" (3.8 cm) wide, length equal to waist measurement.

Cotton string; nylon stocking.

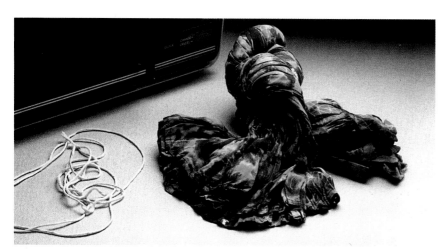

Microwave oven is used to heat-set crinkles in full skirts. The skirt is twisted tightly into a ball and tied with string before it is microwaved.

How to Make a Microwaved Skirt

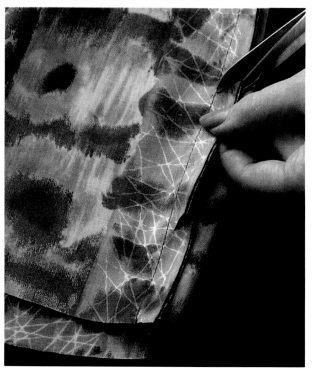

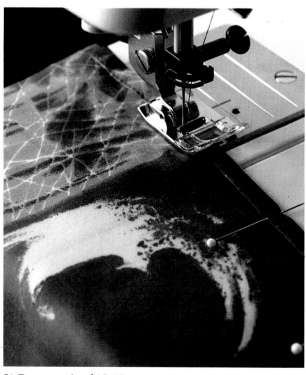

1) Stitch skirt sections, right sides together, matching selvages and stitching narrow seams. Clip selvages diagonally at 4" (10 cm) intervals. Press seams open.

2) Press under ¼" (6 mm) twice on the lower edge of the skirt; stitch to make a double-fold hem.

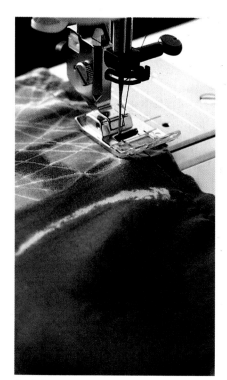

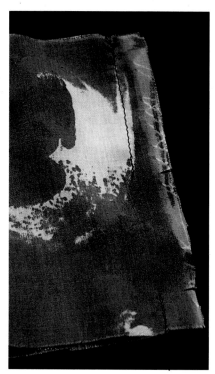

3) Stitch two rows of long straight stitches, ¼" (6 mm) and a scant ½" (1.3 cm) from upper edge of skirt, to be used for gathering.

4) Clip-mark end of waistband at center and ½" (1.3 cm) from one long edge. Stitch ends together in ½" (1.3 cm) seam, leaving opening between marks.

5) Press seam open. Press under ½" (1.3 cm) on long edge of the waistband, on the side opposite the opening.

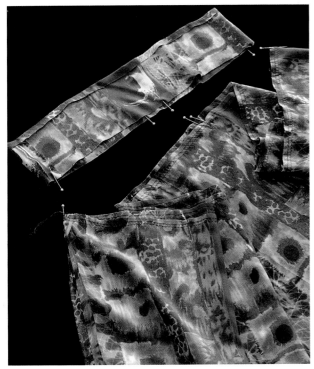

6) Divide upper edge of skirt and unpressed edge of waistband into fourths; pin-mark. Pin waistband to skirt, matching the waistband seam to one skirt seam, with right side of waistband to wrong side of skirt.

7) Pull up threads on upper edge, gathering skirt to fit the waistband. Stitch ½" (1.3 cm) seam. Trim the seam allowance on skirt to ¼" (6 mm). Press seam allowances toward waistband.

8) Fold waistband to right side of the skirt, with pressed edge of the waistband just covering the seam. Topstitch along pressed edge.

9) Dip entire skirt into lukewarm water, soaking fabric thoroughly. Squeeze out excess water.

10) Place the skirt on flat surface, with hem and waistband straight. Beginning at the center of one side, fan-fold across the width of skirt in 1" (2.5 cm) folds.

(Continued on next page)

11) Twist the skirt lengthwise in opposite directions, working with an assistant.

12) Twist the skirt until it is tightly coiled, and wind it into a ball. Wrap and tie cotton string around ball to keep twists from unwinding.

13) Place the twisted ball in microwave oven on an elevated surface. Microwave on low or defrost setting for 4 minutes; allow to rest for 4 minutes.

14) Rotate ¼ turn, and microwave on low or defrost for an additional 4 minutes; allow to rest for 4 minutes. Repeat this process, microwaving a total of five times.

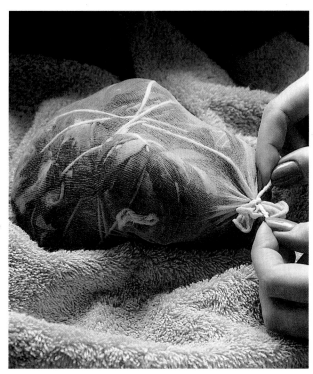

15) **Tie** ball securely into the toe of a nylon stocking; machine dry with towels. Towels absorb moisture and help to reduce noise. It may take more than three hours for ball to dry thoroughly.

16) **Insert** finger into the middle of the ball to test for dryness. When ball is thoroughly dry, untwist; shake out into crinkled pleats.

17) **Insert** elastic into the waistband through opening, using bodkin or safety pin. Pin ends of the elastic together with safety pins.

18) **Try on** skirt, wrong side out. Adjust elastic so it fits comfortably around waist and pulls easily over hips; repin elastic. Cut elastic, allowing for ½" (1.3 cm) overlap. Lap ends, and stitch securely. Stitch opening of waistband closed.

Decorating
T-shirts

Gimp trim, buttons, and pearls decorate the ribbed neckline of this T-shirt.

Lace trim and ribbon roses embellish the hemmed neckline of this T-shirt.

Purchased T-shirts can be given a new, individualized look, with the addition of lace edgings and appliqués, pearlized buttons, or ribbon roses for a neckline accent. And gimp trims at the neckline can be embellished with specialty buttons or charms.

For lace-trimmed T-shirts, select edgings or appliqués from heavier laces, such as Venice lace, which shapes easily as it curves around the neckline. For T-shirts with gimp trims, preshrink the gimp by washing it before it is applied.

To care for a decorated T-shirt, turn it inside out and wash it using the gentle cycle of the machine, or hand wash it, to avoid damaging the trims.

YOU WILL NEED

Purchased T-shirt.
Desired embellishments and trims, such as lace edging, lace appliqués, gimp, buttons, charms, and ribbon roses.

Lace appliqué with openwork embellishes the neckline of a purchased T-shirt, opposite.

Gimp trim and charms are added to the ribbed neckline of this T-shirt.

How to Decorate a T-shirt with a Lace Appliqué

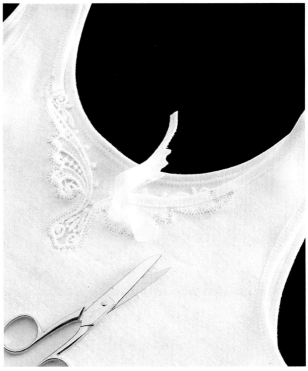

1) Place lace appliqué in the desired position at the neckline, extending the upper edge of appliqué just beyond neck edge. Pin in place.

2) Zigzag along lower edge of appliqué; for openwork, trim fabric under appliqué ⅛" (3 mm) from stitches. If openwork is not desired, zigzag around appliqué.

How to Decorate a T-shirt with Lace Edging and Embellishments

1) Pin lace edging to T-shirt front at lower edge of neckline hem or ribbing; curve lace smoothly, so it lies flat.

2) Machine-stitch lace to T-shirt along inner edge and ends, using long straight stitches. Determine placement of ribbon roses, pearls, or other embellishments; hand-stitch in place through lace and T-shirt.

How to Decorate a T-shirt with Gimp Trim and Embellishments

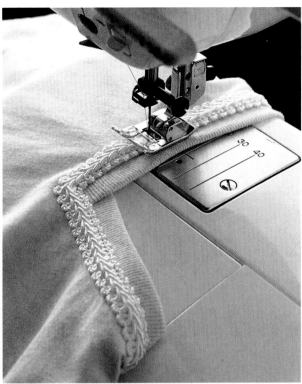

1) Pin gimp trim to T-shirt front at the lower edge of neckline ribbing or hem; curve gimp smoothly, so it lies flat. Fold under ends of gimp at shoulder seams.

2) Machine-stitch gimp to T-shirt along both long edges, using long straight stitches.

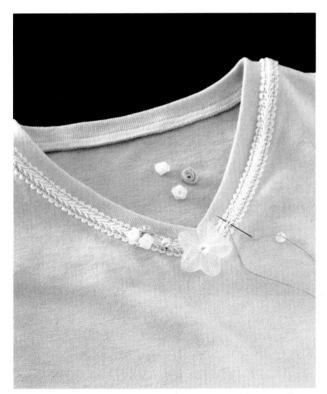

3) Determine placement of buttons, pearls, or other embellishments; hand-stitch in place through gimp and T-shirt.

Gimp and charms. Follow steps 1 and 2, above. Evenly spacing charms on front neckline, hand-stitch each to a single loop on lower edge of gimp.

Slash & Tie T-shirts

A simple slash and tie method adds textural interest to either a purchased T-shirt or one you have made yourself. The slash and tie T-shirt, with its subtle peekaboo effect, requires no sewing.

This design detail can be added to the garment at the lower edge, across the midriff, or to the sleeves. Because this technique will shorten the garment about 4" (10 cm), take this into consideration before you begin.

YOU WILL NEED

T-shirt, either purchased or sewn from a commercial pattern.

How to Sew a Slash and Tie T-shirt

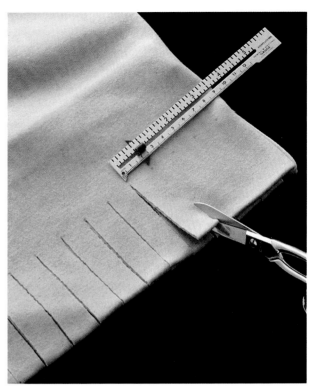

1) Measure distance from lower edge of T-shirt to desired placement of slash detailing. Press under lower edge an amount equal to this measurement plus 2½" (6.5 cm).

2) Place straightedge 2½" (6.5 cm) from pressed fold; mark dots at ¾" (2 cm) intervals. Cut through both layers from fold to marked dots.

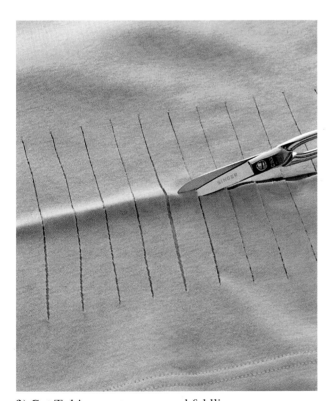

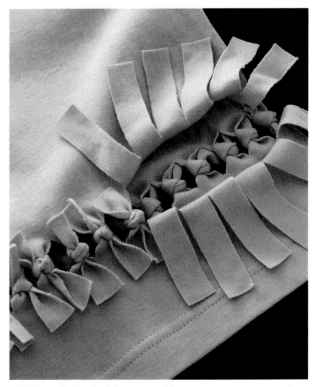

3) Cut T-shirt apart on pressed foldline.

4) Align slashed strips, matching garment seams; tie corresponding strips together, tying all knots in same manner, to create uniform appearance across garment.

Rompers from Secondhand Shirts

These rompers for infants and toddlers are easily made from secondhand or new shirts. Start with either a T-shirt or a button-front shirt in cotton flannel or shirting. For comfort, the rompers have a relaxed fit, and ribbing is used for the cuffs on the sleeves and legs.

For convenient diapering, the rompers fasten along the inseam with a zippered closure. When sewing a romper for an older child, you can eliminate the closure by simply sewing a seam instead.

For the correct fit of the romper, use the chart below to determine the original shirt size to use. Be sure that the original shirt is long enough to provide the desired measurements for the romper.

✂ Cutting Directions

Cut 3½" (9 cm) strips of ribbing on the crosswise grain. From the strips, cut two 5½" (14 cm) lengths for the cuffs on the sleeves and two 6" (15 cm) lengths for the leg openings.

Secondhand shirts can be made into rompers. A button-front shirt was used for the romper above, and a T-shirt for the romper opposite.

YOU WILL NEED

One T-shirt or button-front shirt, size as determined below. **3½" × 23" (9 × 58.5 cm) ribbing.**

One zipper, 16" to 22" (40.5 to 56 cm) in length, depending on size of romper.

Conversion Chart for Sewing Rompers from Shirts

Finished Romper Size	Original Shirt Size	Shoulder to Ankle	Shoulder to Crotch	Chest Width	Back Neck to Wrist
6 to 9 mo.	Child's 6 or 8	22" to 23" (56 to 58.5 cm)	16" to 17" (40.5 to 43 cm)	11" to 12" (28 to 30.5 cm)	10" to 10½" (25.5 to 27.8 cm)
9 to 12 mo.	Child's 10 or 12	23" to 24" (58.5 to 61 cm)	17" to 18" (43 to 46 cm)	12" to 13" (30.5 to 33 cm)	11" to 11½" (28 to 29.3 cm)
12 to 18 mo.	Child's 12 or 14	25" to 27" (63.5 to 68.5 cm)	18" to 18½" (46 to 47.3 cm)	13" to 14" (33 to 35.5 cm)	12" to 13" (30.5 to 33 cm)
18 to 24 mo.	Child's 14 or 16	27" to 28" (68.5 to 71 cm)	19" to 20" (48.5 to 51 cm)	13" to 14" (33 to 35.5 cm)	13" to 14" (33 to 35.5 cm)
2 to 2½ yr.	Men's small or medium	28" to 30" (71 to 76 cm)	19" to 21" (48.5 to 53.5 cm)	13" to 14" (33 to 35.5 cm)	14" to 15" (35.5 to 38 cm)
3 yr.	Men's small or medium	29" to 31" (73.5 to 78.5 cm)	19" to 21" (48.5 to 53.5 cm)	14" to 15" (35.5 to 38 cm)	14" to 15" (35.5 to 38 cm)

How to Sew a Romper from a T-shirt

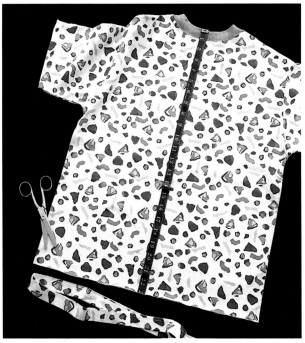

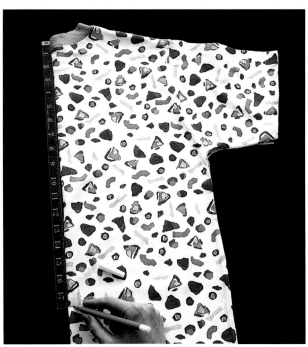

1) Measure shirt from top of ribbing at back neck to desired romper length, according to the chart on page 37. Cut off excess length evenly across shirt.

2) Fold shirt in half, matching sides. Measure from top of ribbing at back neck to desired crotch depth, according to the chart; mark, using a water-soluble marking pen.

3) Mark a point on lower edge, 6" (15 cm) from side seam. Draw line from mark at lower edge to mark at crotch depth, curving line gradually at crotch. Cut away excess fabric through all layers.

4) Measure from center fold at back neck to desired sleeve length, according to chart; mark lower edge of sleeve to this length, perpendicular to upper fold. If sleeve is wider than 6" (15 cm), mark new width 6" (15 cm) from upper fold.

5) Draw new cutting line from mark at lower edge of sleeve, curving slightly toward chest and stopping at point of desired chest width.

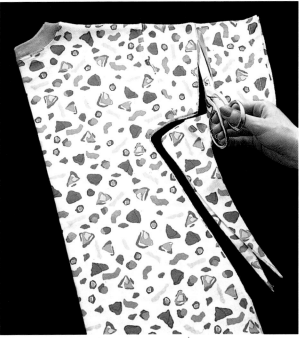

6) Draw new side seam, rounding corner at desired chest width and angling side seam in a gradual curve to original shirt seam, as shown. Cut through all layers along marked lines for sleeve and side seams.

7) Turn garment inside out. On each side of romper, pin the raw edges together for sleeve and side seam; stitch in a continuous seam.

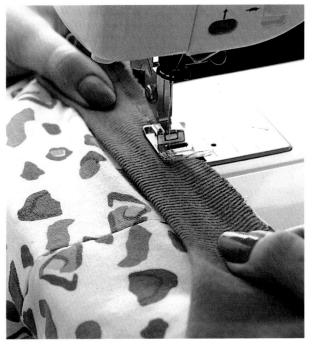

8) Fold one piece of leg ribbing in half lengthwise, *wrong* sides together. Divide ribbing and leg opening in half; pin-mark. Pin ribbing to leg opening, with raw edges even, matching pin marks and ends. Stitch in place ¼" (6 mm) from raw edges, stretching ribbing as you sew. Press seam allowances away from ribbing.

(Continued on next page)

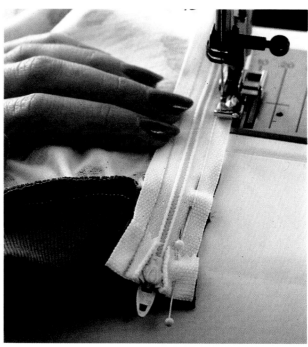

9) Open the zipper. Pin one side of zipper to the back crotch opening, right sides together, with edge of zipper tape along raw edge and top zipper stop near fold of ribbing; fold back upper end of zipper tape. Stitch in place through the center of zipper tape.

10) Close the zipper. Pin other side of zipper tape to front crotch opening, right sides together, aligning seams and ends of opening; fold back upper end of zipper tape. Stitch in place through the center of zipper tape.

11) Make new zipper stop, if zipper is too long, by stitching several times across the zipper teeth 1/2" (1.3 cm) from leg opening. Cut off excess zipper even with leg opening.

12) Stitch the short ends of the remaining piece of leg ribbing together in 1/4" (6 mm) seam; press open. Fold ribbing in half lengthwise, *wrong* sides together. Divide leg opening and ribbing in half; pin-mark.

13) Pin ribbing to leg opening, with raw edges even, matching pin marks and centering ribbing seam on zipper tape. Stitch in place ¼" (6 mm) from raw edges, stretching ribbing as you sew.

14) Prepare ribbing for sleeves as in step 12. Pin ribbing to sleeve opening, with raw edges even, matching pin marks and seams. Stitch in place ¼" (6 mm) from raw edges, stretching ribbing as you sew. Press the seam allowances away from ribbing.

How to Sew a Romper from a Button-front Shirt

1) Button the shirt. Measure shirt from neckline seam, below collar, to desired romper length, according to the chart on page 37. Cut off excess length evenly across the shirt. Follow steps 2 and 3 on page 38, measuring for crotch depth from the neckline seam, below collar.

2) Follow steps 4 to 9; finish seams after step 7, using zigzag or overlock stitch. Baste fronts together across placket on lower edge. Apply zipper to crotch front as in step 10, stitching through all layers of basted placket. Complete garment as in steps 11 to 14.

Puppy Bath Ponchos

Make this cuddly after-bath poncho for your child from two bath towels. The instructions that follow are for a puppy poncho. By changing the ears and facial features, you can make a poncho that looks like a bunny or a kitty. Prewash the towels and fabrics to preshrink them.

✂ Cutting Directions

From one towel, cut a 10" × 22" (25.5 × 56 cm) rectangle for the hood, with one long edge along the selvage of the towel. From the same towel, cut two ear pieces and two foot pieces, using the patterns on page 47. From contrasting fabric, cut two ear pieces and two foot pieces. From scraps of black broadcloth, cut the pieces for the nose and eyes as in step 2, below.

YOU WILL NEED

Two bath towels, about 25" × 50" (63.5 × 127 cm) in size.

¼ yd. (0.25 m) contrasting fabric, such as plaid or animal-print cotton flannel or broadcloth, for ears and feet.

Scraps of black broadcloth, for eyes and nose.

Paper-backed fusible web.

Tear-away stabilizer.

How to Sew a Puppy Bath Poncho

1) **Fold** hood piece in half along selvage. On the side opposite the selvage, use a saucer to round corner from fold to raw edges.

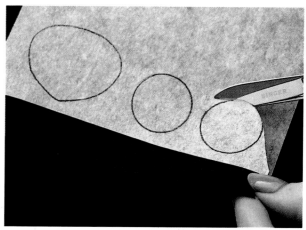

2) **Fuse** paper-backed fusible web to wrong side of black broadcloth; using patterns on page 46, trace eyes and nose onto paper side. Cut out pieces.

(Continued on next page)

3) Remove the paper backing from the eyes and nose. Pin-mark center of hood at selvage. Following placement guide on page 46, fuse pieces to hood.

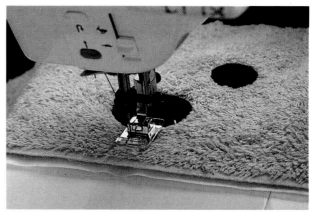

4) Set machine for satin stitching by adjusting zigzag stitch for closely spaced, wide stitches. Satin-stitch around eyes and nose, placing tear-away stabilizer under hood; satin-stitch the mouth as shown on the placement guide (page 46).

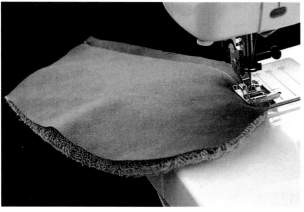

5) Place one ear piece from terry cloth and one from contrasting fabric right sides together. Stitch ³⁄₈" (1 cm) seam around curved edge, leaving the straight end unstitched; clip curves. Turn right side out. Repeat for remaining ear and both feet.

6) Place one ear, contrasting side down, with straight end on placement line and with ear lying above face. Stitch in place along the open end, using wide, short zigzag stitches. Repeat for other ear.

7) Fold the hood in half, with right sides together, matching raw edges. Stitch ³⁄₈" (1 cm) center back seam on the curved side of the hood; finish seam, using zigzag or overlock stitch.

8) Fold remaining bath towel in half, with lower edge of top layer 1" (2.5 cm) above lower edge of bottom layer. Mark the center of the fold; on fold, measure and mark 5¼" (13.2 cm) on each side of center.

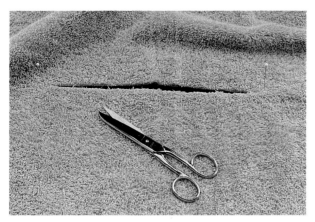

9) **Unfold** the bath towel. Slash the towel between the end markings, for a 10½" (27.8 cm) opening.

10) **Pin** the hood to the towel at opening, right sides together; match the center back seam of the hood to center marking on longer side of towel. Front edges of hood will not meet.

11) **Stitch** hood to body in ⅜" (1 cm) seam. Zigzag or overlock seam allowances together, continuing across the slash between edges of hood in front.

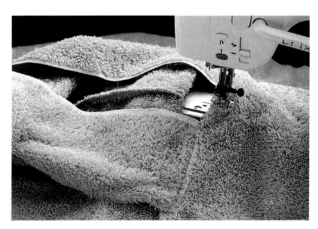

12) **Fold** seam allowances toward the body. Topstitch through all layers, ¼" (6 mm) from the seamline; continue stitching across the front opening.

13) **Pin** feet, contrasting sides down, to wrong side of towel front, at lower edge and 6" (15 cm) from sides; overlap edges ½" (1.3 cm).

14) **Stitch,** using short, wide zigzag stitches. Topstitch through all layers, ¼" (6 mm) from the lower edge of the towel.

Placement Guide and Patterns for a Puppy Bath Poncho

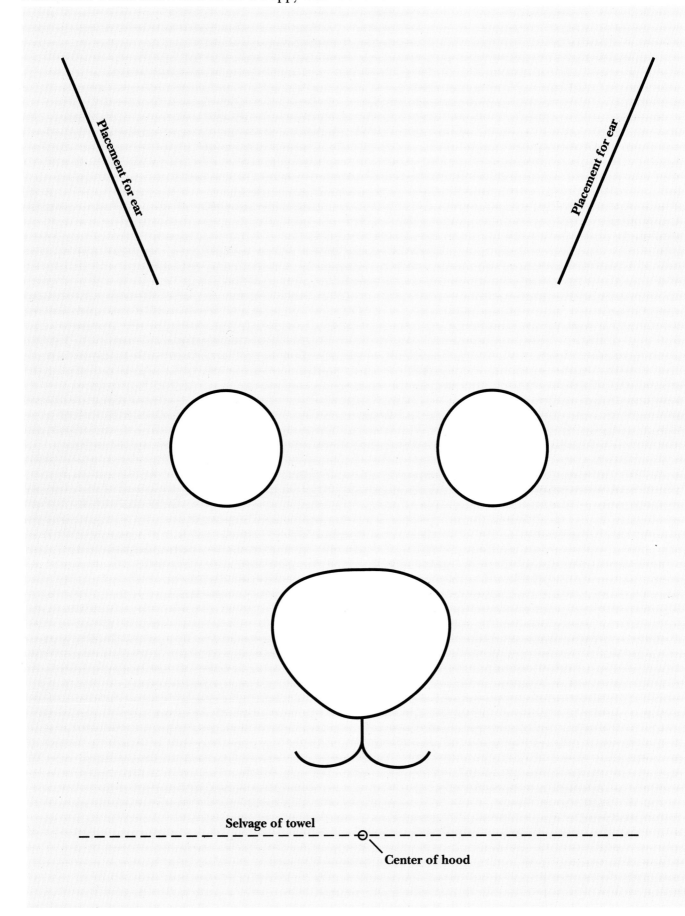

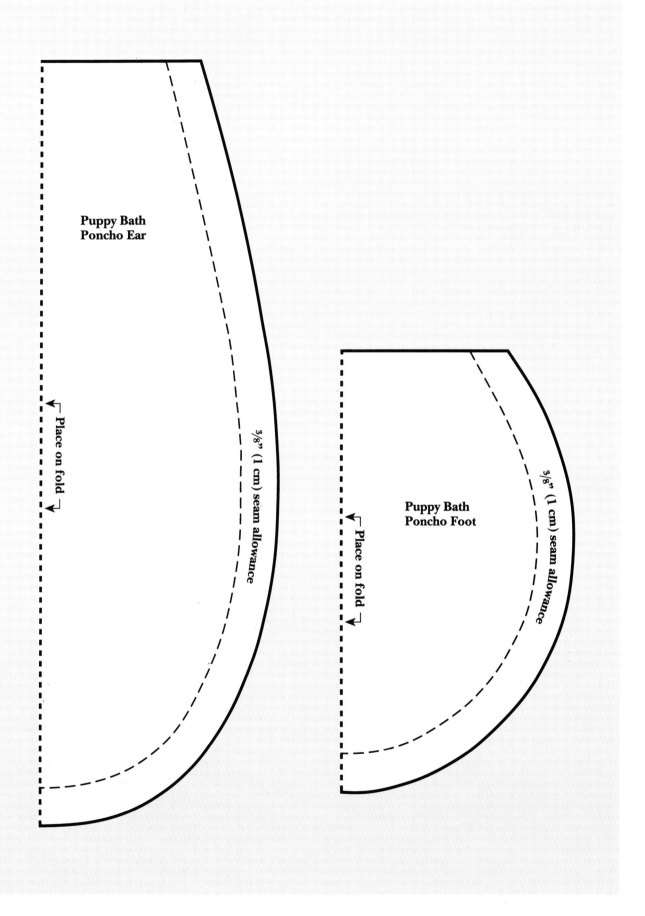

Puppy Bath
Poncho Ear

Place on fold

3/8" (1 cm) seam allowance

Puppy Bath
Poncho Foot

Place on fold

3/8" (1 cm) seam allowance

Quick Accessories

Envelope Purses

This simple envelope purse has a generous flap and a shoulder strap of decorative cording. For evening wear, select an elegant fabric, such as brocade, velveteen, or satin. For a casual look, select denim, poplin, or a decorator fabric.

To add a decorative touch to an envelope purse, the fabric may be embellished with fabric painting or decorative studs before the purse is sewn.

For a painted purse, remove any sizing from the fabric by washing it before you begin the project. If you are unfamiliar with using fabric paints, you may want to practice the painting techniques on scraps of the fabric before you paint on the fabric piece for the purse. Heat-set the paints according to the manufacturer's directions; usually paints are heat-set by pressing the painted fabric with an iron.

Decorative studs may be used alone or in combination with fabric painting. Simple to apply, the studs are secured to the fabric by pressing their pointed legs through the fabric, then bending the legs inward.

✂ Cutting Directions

Cut one 7" × 22" (18 × 56 cm) rectangle each from the outer fabric and the lining.

YOU WILL NEED

¼ yd. (0.25 m) each of outer fabric and lining, if fabric will be cut on crosswise grain; or ¾ yd. (0.7 m) each, if cut on lengthwise grain.

1½ yd. (1.4 m) decorative cording.

Fabric paints and synthetic brushes, if desired.

Decorative studs, if desired.

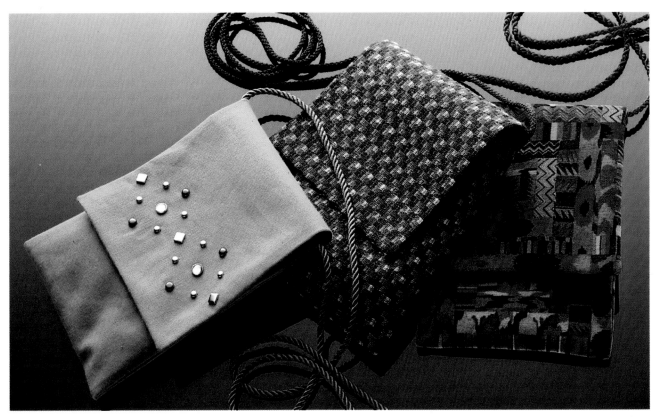

Envelope purses (shown left to right) are embellished with decorative studs and sewn from textured cotton and printed velvet. The purse opposite is embellished with fabric paints.

How to Embellish the Purse Fabric with Fabric Paints

1) Protect work surface with brown paper. Tape 7" × 22" (18 × 56 cm) rectangle of outer fabric to brown paper, placing tape ¼" (6 mm) from raw edges. Using synthetic brush, apply 1" to 1½" (2.5 to 3.8 cm) stripes of paint in desired colors. Allow to dry.

2) Paint designs across each stripe, in zigzag patterns, swirls, and simple geometric shapes. Allow to dry. Remove tape carefully from edges of fabric.

How to Embellish the Purse Fabric with Decorative Studs

1) Mark design placement for studs on right side of fabric. Press pointed legs of studs through fabric to wrong side; work carefully, because points are sharp.

2) Place fabric, right side down, on firm work surface; bend legs inward, using the handle of a spoon, to secure studs.

How to Sew an Envelope Purse

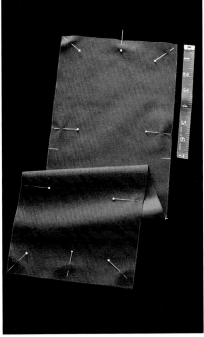

1) Pin the outer fabric and lining, right sides together. For the flap, mark points on both long sides, 7" (18 cm) from one short end.

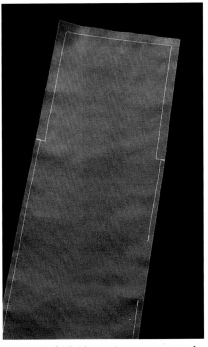

2) Stitch ¼" (6 mm) seam around lower portion of purse, starting at one side. Pivot at markings; stitch ½" (1.3 cm) seam around flap. Continue ¼" (6 mm) seam on lower portion; stop 3" (7.5 cm) from starting point, for opening.

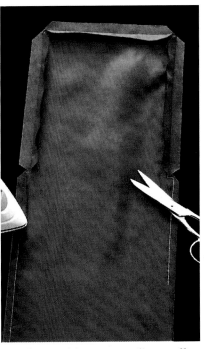

3) Trim outside corners diagonally; notch inside corners. Press seam open, with lining side of the purse facing up.

4) Turn purse right side out; press. Slipstitch opening closed.

5) Fold lower 7" (18 cm) of purse to flap, right sides together. Stitch ¼" (6 mm) side seams.

6) Zigzag the cording to the seam allowances on each side of purse, catching the end of cording for 1" (2.5 cm). Turn the purse right side out, folding the flap down.

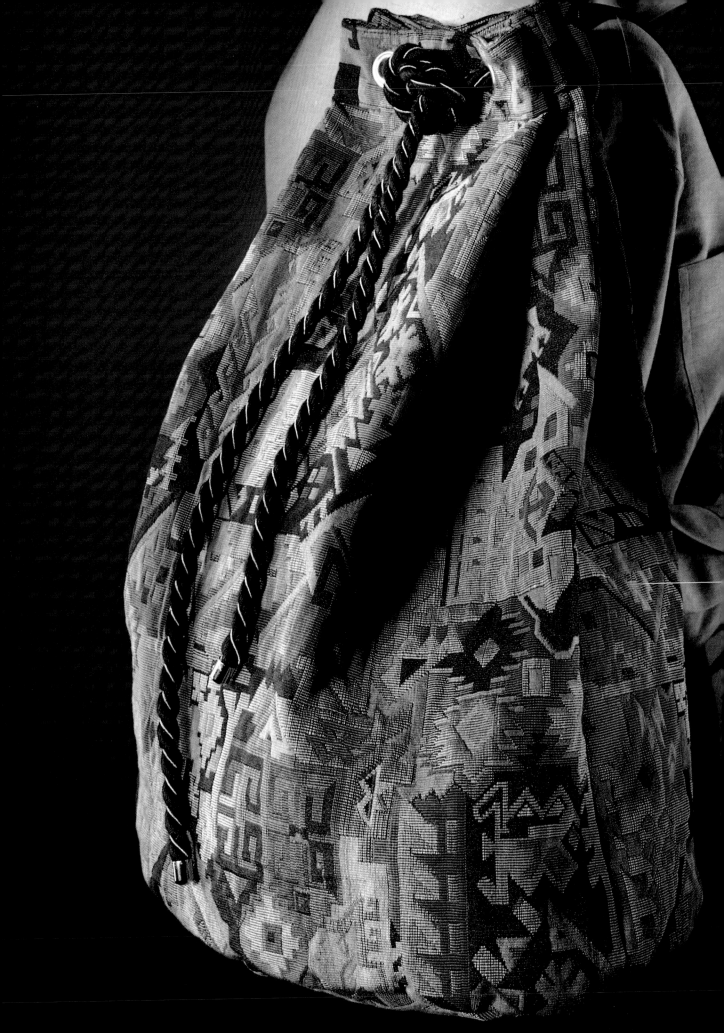

Drawstring Duffle Bags

This versatile duffle bag is an attractive and practical tote. It features an adjustable shoulder strap and a grommet-and-cording closure. The bag expands to a generous capacity, yet the top draws closed in neat folds.

The duffle bag may be made from decorator fabric, tapestry, or denim. Mediumweight fabrics are the easiest to sew; extremely heavy or stiff fabrics are often difficult to handle.

Either nylon or cotton webbing may be used for the shoulder strap. If nylon webbing is used, seal the cut ends of the webbing to prevent raveling. This is done by holding the ends near a flame until the nylon fibers melt and bond together, as shown in step 3 on page 57. If cotton webbing is used, it is not necessary to seal the cut ends.

The bottom of the duffle bag uses an oval pattern, measuring 11" × 15½" (28 × 39.3 cm). To make an oval this size, use the simple string-and-pencil technique on page 56.

✂ Cutting Directions

For the bottom of the duffle bag, cut one oval from fabric, using the oval pattern on page 56. For the body of the bag, cut one rectangle from fabric, 21" × 41½" (53.5 × 105.3 cm). For the upper band of the bag, cut one fabric strip, 2½" × 41½" (6.5 × 105.3 cm).

YOU WILL NEED

1 yd. (0.95 m) fabric, 45" (115 cm) wide; or ⅔ yd. (0.63 m) fabric, 54" to 60" (137 to 152.5 cm) wide.

1¼ yd. (1.15 m) webbing, 1" or 1½" (2.5 or 3.8 cm) wide, for shoulder strap.

One rectangular ring in same width as webbing.

One slide or two-sided buckle without prong, in same width as webbing.

Twelve ½" (1.3 cm) grommets; attaching tool for grommets.

1½ yd. (1.4 m) heavy twisted cording, for drawstring.

Two end caps, for cording, optional.

How to Make an Oval Pattern for a Drawstring Duffle Bag

1) Insert two push pins into cardboard, 15½" (39.3 cm) apart. Knot string around one push pin. Loop string around other push pin, pulling it tight; tie knot, making sure string remains taut.

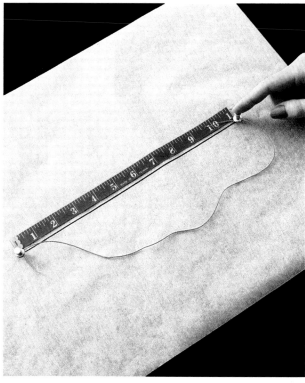

2) Remove push pins with string from cardboard. Draw 11" (28 cm) line on sheet of paper. Insert push pins at ends of line, into paper and cardboard.

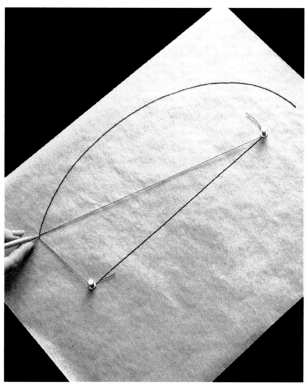

3) Pull the string taut with point of a pencil, keeping string close to paper surface. Draw upper half of the oval, keeping string taut as pencil slides along string.

4) Move pencil to opposite side of string; draw lower half of oval in same manner.

56

How to Sew a Drawstring Duffle Bag

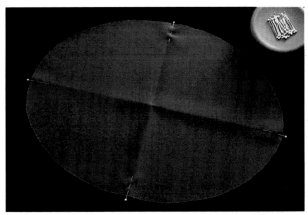

1) Stitch short sides of bag body, right sides together, in ¼" (6 mm) seam. Zigzag or overlock the seam allowances together; press seam to one side. Fold and pin-mark lower edge of bag body into fourths, with one pin at side seam; repeat for upper edge.

2) Fold the fabric oval for the bottom of the bag in half lengthwise and crosswise; pin-mark fabric into fourths at folds.

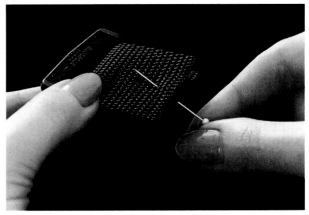

3) Cut one 3" (7.5 cm) length of webbing. If nylon webbing is used, seal the cut ends of the webbing to prevent raveling, by holding each end near a flame until the nylon fibers melt and bond together.

4) Thread 3" (7.5 cm) strip of sealed webbing through rectangular ring. Pin ends together.

5) Pin webbing piece from step 4 to lower edge of bag body, centering it over the first pin mark away from side seam. Secure webbing to fabric with two rows of stitching, ¼" and ⅛" (6 and 3 mm) from edge.

6) Seal one end of remaining length of nylon webbing; slip sealed end around center bar of slide or buckle. Fold back the end; stitch in place, ¼" and ⅛" (6 and 3 mm) from edge.

(Continued on next page)

How to Sew a Drawstring Duffle Bag (continued)

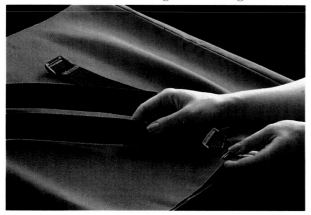

7) **Lay** bag body right side up. With strap wrong side up, pull free end of strap under and through rectangular ring as shown.

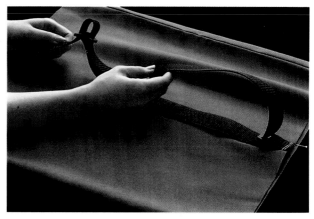

8) **Fold** the strap back against itself. Pull the end of the strap in and out of the slide.

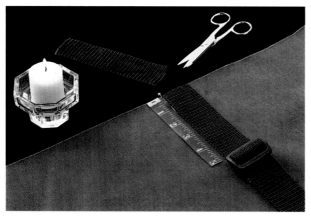

9) **Adjust** the slide so it is 5" (12.5 cm) from upper edge of bag body, with strap lying flat on bag. Trim excess webbing even with the upper edge of the bag; seal the end.

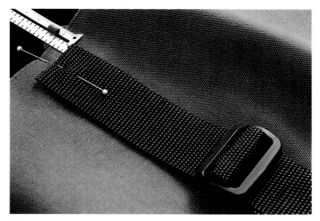

10) **Pin** strap to top of bag body, centering it at pin mark, with edge of strap ½" (1.3 cm) from upper edge of bag. Stitch in place ¼" and ⅛" (6 and 3 mm) from edge of strap.

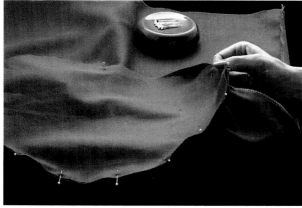

11) **Pin** fabric oval to bag body, right sides together, with side seam at pin mark on narrow end of oval. Match the remaining pin marks.

12) **Stitch** ½" (1.3 cm) seam around bottom of bag, stitching with bag body facing up. Stretch or ease oval to fit the bag body, if necessary. Zigzag or overlock the seam allowances together.

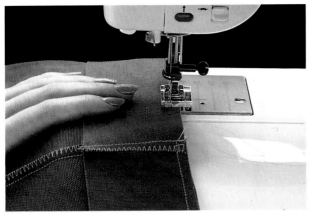

13) Stitch ends of upper band, right sides together, in ¼" (6 mm) seam; zigzag or overlock seam allowances together, and press to one side. Pin band to upper edge of bag, with right side of band against wrong side of bag; match side seams, and turn seam allowances in opposite directions. Stitch ¼" (6 mm) seam.

14) Press seam open. Fold under ¼" (6 mm) on the unfinished edge of the band; press.

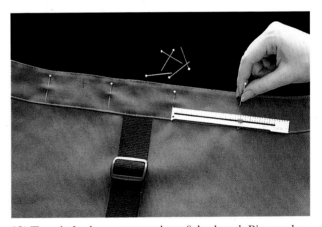

15) Turn bag right side out. Press band to right side of bag; pin in place. Stitch band to bag along folded edge. Stitch over strap a second time, to reinforce it.

16) Topstitch along upper edge of the band. Pin-mark the placement for 12 grommets, evenly spacing them about 3⅜" (8.5 cm) apart, with first two grommets positioned an equal distance on either side of strap.

17) Attach grommets in center of band at placement markings, following manufacturer's directions.

18) Insert cording through grommet next to center front of bag. Weave cording in and out; apply end caps to cording, if desired.

Fleece Accessories

Fleece, such as Polartec®, is a warm, washable fabric that can be used to create outdoor winter accessories for the entire family. Because the fleece is available in a wide selection of bright colors, these items make fun fashion accents. Mix and match an assortment of scarves, neckwarmers, and headwarmers, each made from a single piece of fabric. To complete the accessory wardrobe, make easy-to-sew mittens, custom-fitted to each person's hand measurements. Synthetic suede can be added to the palms of the mittens, if desired, for a better grip.

✂ Cutting Directions

For an adult's scarf, cut one 12" × 60" (30.5 × 152.5 cm) strip of fleece crosswise on the fabric; or, for a child's scarf, cut one 10" (25.5 cm) strip.

To determine the lengths of the fabric strips for the neckwarmer and headband, measure the circumference of your head, using a tape measure. For an adult's neckwarmer, cut one 10" (25.5 cm) strip of fleece crosswise on the fabric, with the length of the strip ½" (1.3 cm) shorter than your head size; or, for a child's size, cut one 8" (20.5 cm) strip.

For an adult's or child's headband, make a pattern as on page 63, steps 1 and 2. Cut one piece of fleece crosswise on the fabric, using the pattern.

For an adult's mittens, make a pattern as on page 64, steps 1 to 3. Using the pattern as a guide, cut the fabric, elastic, and suede as in steps 4 to 6. For a child's mittens, follow the easy variations on page 65.

YOU WILL NEED

⅓ **yd. (0.32 m) fleece,** 60"
(152.5 cm) wide, for scarf.

⅜ **yd. (0.35 m) fleece,** for adult's
neckwarmer, or ¼ yd. (0.25 m)
for child's neckwarmer.

⅛ **yd. (0,15 m) fleece,** for
headwarmer.

⅓ **yd. (0.32 m) fleece,** for
mittens.

¼ **yd. (0.25 m) elastic,** ⅜"
(1 cm) wide, for mittens.

Synthetic suede, two 2" × 5"
(5 × 12.5 cm) scraps, optional
for mittens.

How to Sew a Fleece Scarf

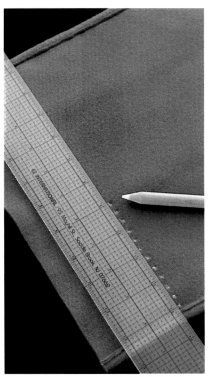

1) Cut fleece as on page 60. Fold ⅜" (1 cm) to wrong side on long edges of fabric strip for scarf; stitch close to raw edges.

2) Lay a ruler across one narrow end of scarf, 3" (7.5 cm) from raw edge. Using chalk pencil, mark fabric at ⅜" (1 cm) intervals, beginning at inner edge of side hems.

3) Move ruler to raw edge; mark as in step 2. Cut slashes from outer marks to inner marks, making the fringe. Repeat at other end of scarf.

How to Sew a Fleece Neckwarmer

1) Cut fleece as on page 60. Stitch narrow ends of fabric strip together in ¼" (6 mm) seam.

2) Fold ⅜" (1 cm) to wrong side on the long edges; stitch close to raw edges.

How to Sew a Fleece Headband

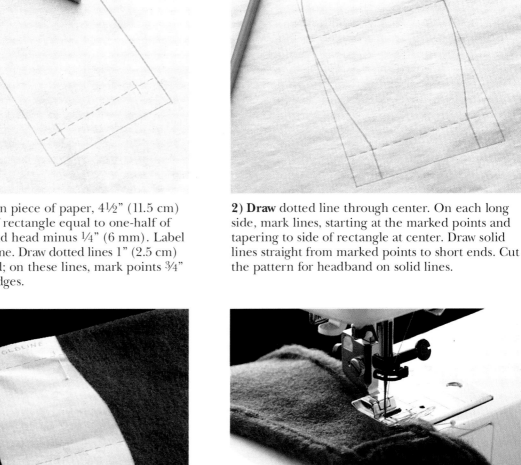

1) Draw rectangle on piece of paper, 4½" (11.5 cm) wide, with length of rectangle equal to one-half of measurement around head minus ¼" (6 mm). Label one end as the foldline. Draw dotted lines 1" (2.5 cm) from each short end; on these lines, mark points ¾" (2 cm) from long edges.

2) Draw dotted line through center. On each long side, mark lines, starting at the marked points and tapering to side of rectangle at center. Draw solid lines straight from marked points to short ends. Cut the pattern for headband on solid lines.

3) Fold fleece lengthwise; using pattern, cut fleece, with foldline of pattern on fold of fabric.

4) Stitch narrow ends of fabric strip together in ¼" (6 mm) seam. Fold ⅜" (1 cm) to wrong side on long edges; stitch close to raw edges.

How to Sew Adult's Fleece Mittens

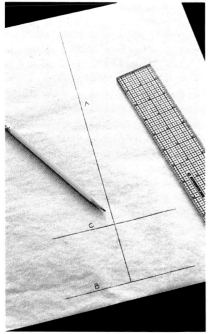

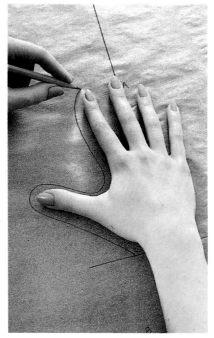

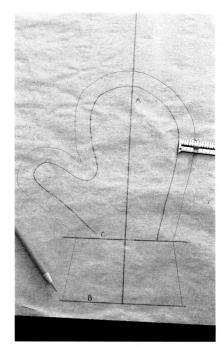

1) Draw a line on tracing paper, about 15" (38 cm) long. Draw 6" (15 cm) line at end of first line and another 3" (7.5 cm) from the same end; lines should be perpendicular to and centered on first line. Label the lines A, B, and C as shown.

2) Place hand on tracing paper, with middle finger on Line A and with wrist centered on Line C. Fingers should be slightly spread, with thumb extended out to the side, as shown. Draw around hand, beginning and ending at Line C.

3) Draw cutting lines ¾" (2 cm) outside the hand markings, to allow for ease and seam allowances. Extend cutting lines from Line C to Line B, angling lines so Line B measures 1" (2.5 cm) wider than Line C, between cutting lines.

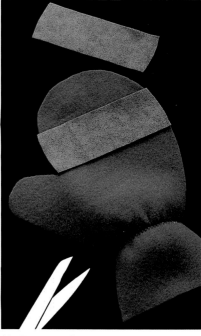

4) Fold fleece right sides together; cut four mitten pieces from fleece, with crosswise direction of fabric across palm. Using chalk, mark Line C on wrong side of two opposite mitten pieces.

5) Cut two lengths of elastic, each 1" (2.5 cm) shorter than Line C. Stretch one length to fit Line C on wrong side of mitten piece; stitch, using zigzag stitch. Repeat for the opposite mitten piece.

6) Cut two 2" (5 cm) strips of synthetic suede, if desired, with width of strips equal to width of mitten above thumb.

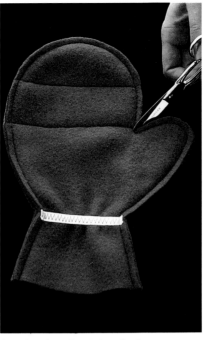

7) Apply synthetic suede pieces to elasticized mitten pieces, using a glue stick; position strip parallel to Lines B and C. Edgestitch in place on long edges.

8) Pin the elasticized pieces to the remaining pieces, right sides together, matching Lines B and C. Stitch ¼" (6 mm) seam around mittens, leaving ends open. Clip corner at thumb.

9) Turn the mittens right side out. Fold under a ½" (1.3 cm) hem allowance at the mitten openings. Stitch hems, using zigzag stitch.

How to Sew Child's Fleece Mittens

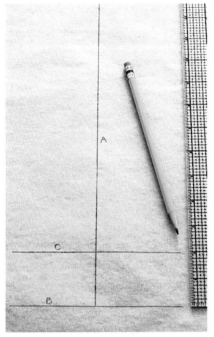

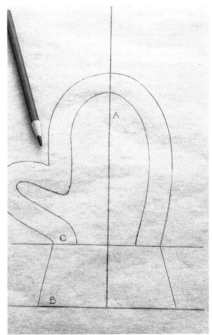

1) Follow step 1, opposite, for making mitten pattern, except draw Line C about 2" (5 cm) from Line B.

2) Follow steps 2 and 3, opposite, except in step 3, extend cutting lines so Line B measures ¾" (2 cm) wider than Line C.

3) Sew mittens as in steps 4 to 9, using narrower strips of synthetic suede, if desired.

Gripper-tread fabric is used for nonslip soles on booties.

Fleece Booties

Cozy, roomy booties made from fleece, such as Polartec®, are great for a quick warm-up after a day on the ski slopes or for lounging around the house on chilly evenings. With the instructions that follow, you can make fleece booties for adults and children. For nonslip soles, a special gripper-tread fabric is used.

✄ Cutting Directions
Make the patterns for the booties as in steps 1 to 7, below. For each pair of booties, cut two upper pieces from the outer fabric. From the lining, cut two

upper pieces and two soles. From the gripper-tread fabric, cut two soles. From the cording, cut two ties, each 16" (40.5 cm) long.

YOU WILL NEED

¼ **yd. (0.25 m) fleece,** for outer fabric.

¼ **yd. (0.25 m) fleece,** for lining.

¼ **yd. (0.25 m) gripper-tread fabric,** for soles.

1 yd. (0.95 m) cording, for tie.

How to Sew Fleece Booties

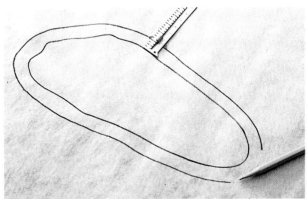

1) Make pattern for bootie sole by drawing around foot onto piece of tracing paper; draw cutting line ½" (1.3 cm) outside the foot marking, to allow for ease and seam allowances. Round the pattern in the toe area.

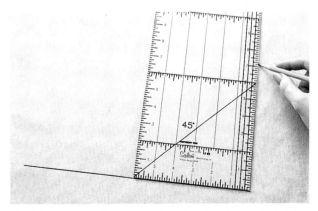

2) Make pattern for upper piece by drawing a straight line for lower edge, 1" (2.5 cm) longer than the sole pattern. For back foldline, draw perpendicular line at one end of lower edge, 7¼" (18.7 cm) long for adult size or 6" (15 cm) long for child size.

(Continued on next page)

How to Sew Fleece Booties (continued)

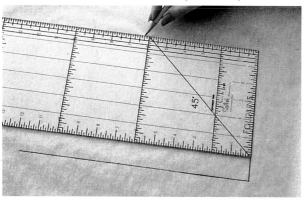

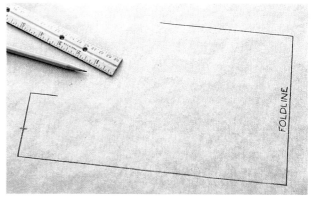

3) Draw a line for top opening of bootie, parallel to lower edge and starting at the upper end of the back foldline; draw this line 6¼" (15.7 cm) long for adult size or 5" (12.5 cm) long for child size.

4) Draw line at toe end, perpendicular to lower edge, 3" (7.5 cm) long for adult size or 2½" (6.5 cm) for child size. Mark a point 1¾" (4.5 cm) down from upper end of line for adult size or 1½" (3.8 cm) from end for child size. Draw line from upper end of this line toward back foldline, 1¼" (3.2 cm) for all sizes.

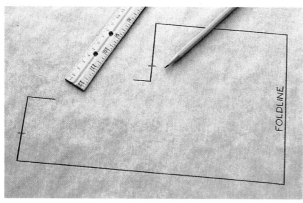

5) Draw a line down from the end of top opening, 3" (7.5 cm) long for adult size or 2¼" (6 cm) for child size. Mark a point ¾" (2 cm) up from bottom of this line for adult size or ⅝" (1 cm) for child size. Draw horizontal line from bottom of this line toward toe end, same length as line from marked point.

6) Round the corner at toe as shown, using saucer. Round the corner at top of foot as shown, using a water glass.

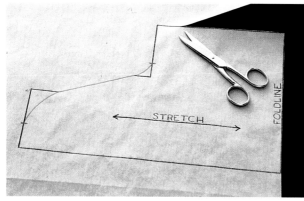

7) Draw straight line between toe curve and upper curve. Cut out pattern, following curved lines on front. Mark the direction of greatest fabric stretch, parallel to lower edge.

8) Cut out fabric as on page 67. Stitch ¼" (6 mm) center front seam in upper piece from outer fabric, right sides together. Repeat for remaining outer bootie and for bootie linings. Press seams open.

9) Pin one outer bootie to one bootie lining, right sides together, matching center front seams. Stitch ¼" (6 mm) seam around top opening. Repeat for other bootie. Press seams open.

10) Turn bootie right side out; topstitch ⅜" (1 cm) from top opening seam. Baste the lower edges of outer fabric and lining together, within ¼" (6 mm) seam allowances.

11) Center cording for tie over front seam, at upper curve. Stitch to bootie, using short zigzag stitches; begin and end 1" (2.5 cm) on either side of front seam. Knot ends of cording; tie into bow.

12) Place one outer sole and one sole lining wrong sides together. Baste a scant ¼" (6 mm) from outer edge. Repeat for remaining outer sole and lining.

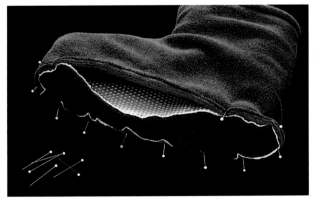

13) Turn bootie lining side out. Pin sole to bootie, outer sides together, centering sole at front seamline and center back; ease in excess fullness. Stitch ¼" (6 mm) seam, with sole side down.

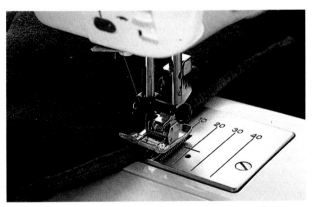

14) Trim the seam allowance on the outer sole to ⅛" (3 mm). Zigzag or overlock the seam allowances together around bootie. Turn bootie right side out.

Fun Toys to Sew

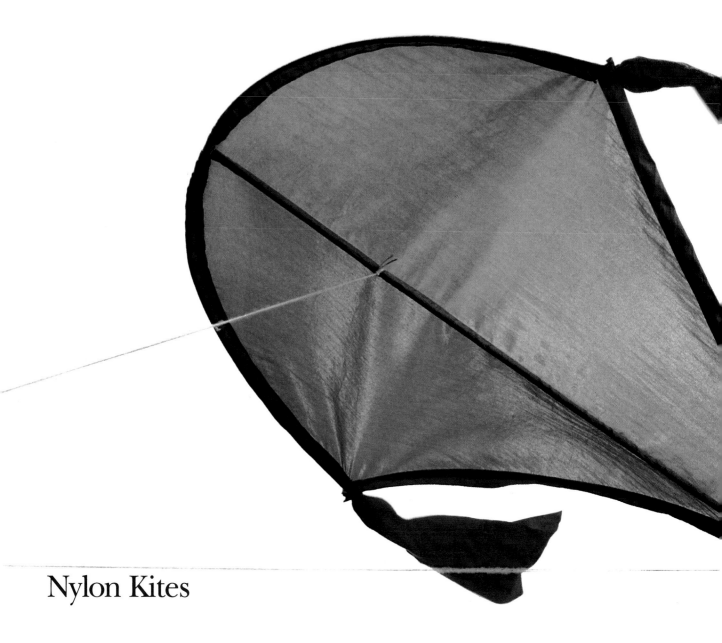

Nylon Kites

Kites are fun both to make and to fly. The two styles of kites shown here are simple to sew, inexpensive, and fly easily. Because each has its own appeal, you may want to make them both, in brilliant colors.

These kites fit into two different categories: delta and flexible. Delta kites, like the fringed delta kite opposite, are generally triangular in shape and have

four spars, or dowels: two along the wing edges, a spine down the middle, and a spreader. By removing the spreader, you can fold the kite for easy storage.

Flexible kites, like the arch-top flexible kite above, are designed to bend, even in light winds, helping them remain stable. This flexible kite has an arched spar and a spine.

YOU WILL NEED

For a fringed delta kite:
1 yd. (0.95 m) nylon fabric, 45" or 60" (115 or 152.5 cm) wide, for sail and keel.
One ¼" **(6 mm) dowel,** 21½" (54.8 cm) long, for spine.
One ¼" **(6 mm) dowel,** 19½" (49.8 cm) long, for spreader.
Two ³⁄₁₆" **(4.5 mm) dowels,** each 26¾" (68 cm) long, for wing spars.
Two caps from ballpoint pens.
Eyelet; kite line.

For an arch-top flexible kite:
¾ **yd. (0.7 m) nylon fabric,** 45" or 60" (115 or 152.5 cm) wide, for sail.
1¼ **yd. (1.15 m) nylon fabric,** for tails; this is sufficient yardage for all tails.
⅝ **yd. (0.6 m) nylon fabric,** optional second color for tails at sides of kite.
One ⅛" **(3 mm) dowel,** 30" (76 cm) long, for spar.
One ³⁄₁₆" **(4.5 mm) dowel,** 23½" (59.8 cm) long, for spar.
Kite line.

✂ Cutting Directions

For a fringed delta kite, make the patterns for the sail and keel, opposite. Fold nylon fabric on the bias; cut one sail, using the pattern, placing the foldline of the pattern on a bias fold of the fabric. Cut two fabric triangles for the keel, using the pattern, with the 13" (33 cm) side on the lengthwise grain. For the spreader tabs, cut one 1½" × 6" (3.8 × 15 cm) strip of fabric.

For an arch-top flexible kite, make the pattern for the sail as on page 78. Fold the nylon fabric on the lengthwise grain; cut one sail, using the pattern, placing the foldline of the pattern on the lengthwise fold of the fabric. Cut 2" (5 cm) strips on the bias, for tails. You will need two 5-ft. (1.58 m) tails for the lower point of the kite and two 28" (71 cm) tails for the sides of the kite.

Parts of a Kite

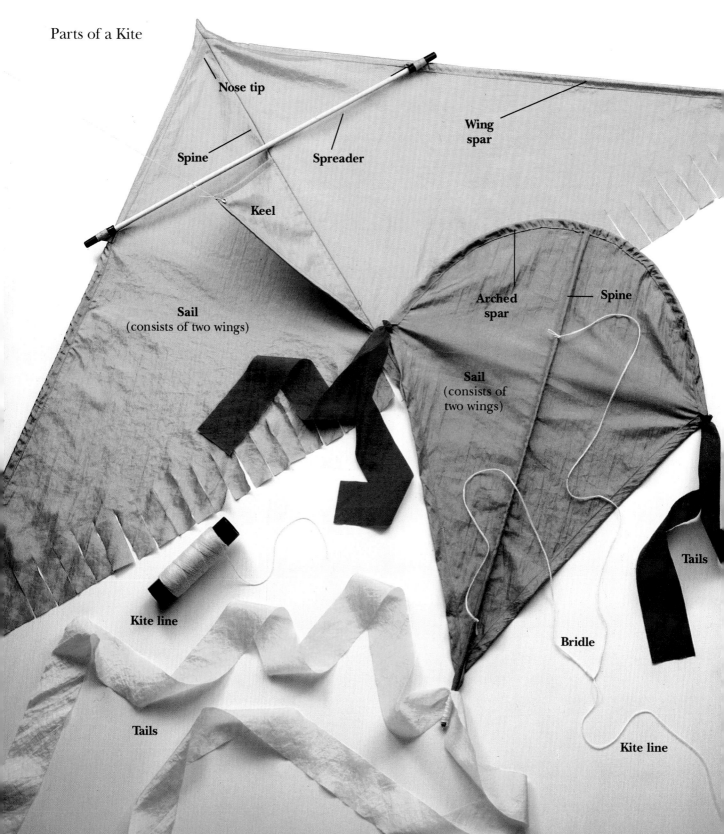

How to Make the Patterns for a Fringed Delta Kite

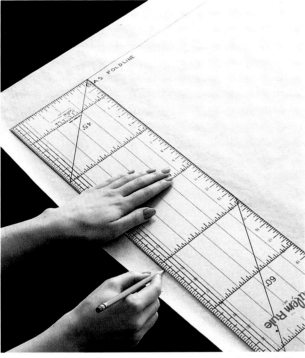

1) Draw 22½" (57.3 cm) line on paper, using pencil; label line as bias foldline. At lower end of line, mark a perpendicular 24" (61 cm) line.

2) Draw 2½" (6.5 cm) line, using pencil, up from and perpendicular to 24" (61 cm) line.

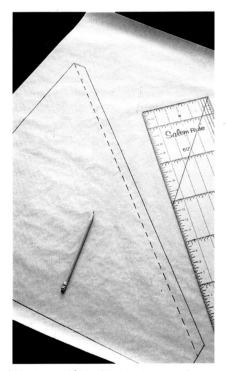

3) Draw 31¼" (79.1 cm) dotted line, connecting upper end of 2½" (6.5 cm) line and upper end of bias foldline. Draw cutting line, ¾" (2 cm) from dotted line, to allow for wing spar casing. This pattern is for sail of kite.

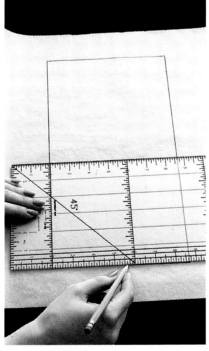

4) Draw 6⅝" × 13" (16.5 × 33 cm) rectangle on paper.

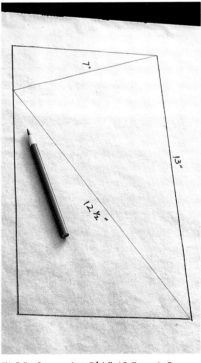

5) Mark a point 2½" (6.5 cm) from corner, on 13" (33 cm) side. Draw lines from this point to corners on opposite side of rectangle, to make a triangular pattern for keel, 7" × 12½" × 13" (18 × 31.8 × 33 cm).

How to Make a Fringed Delta Kite

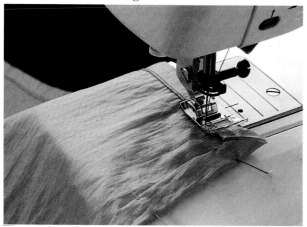

1) Make casings for the wing spars by turning under ¼" (6 mm), then ½" (1.3 cm) on 31¼" (79.1 cm) wing edges.

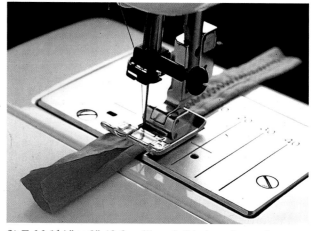

2) Stitch the keel pieces together along 7" and 12½" (18 and 31.8 cm) sides, stitching ½" (1.3 cm) seams. Trim corners; turn keel right side out. Topstitch ¼" (6 mm) from seamed edges, to reinforce.

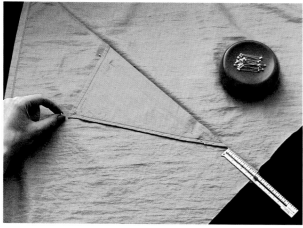

3) Fold sail in half on foldline; press. Align raw edge of keel to pressed fold, with narrow point of keel 2½" (6.5 cm) from lower edge of sail; pin in place.

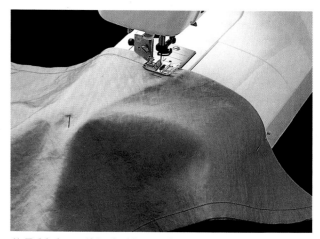

4) Fold the sail in half, matching the wing edges and enclosing keel; secure keel by pinning along foldline. Stitch from lower edge of sail to nose tip, ½" (1.3 cm) from foldline, to make casing for spine.

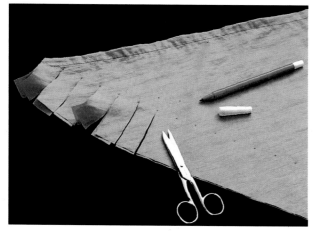

5) Place straightedge 2½" (6.5 cm) from lower edge; Mark dots at 1" (2.5 cm) intervals. Cut the fringe by slashing the sail from lower edge to marked dots.

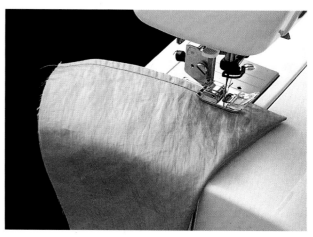

6) Fold 1¼" × 6" (3.8 × 15 cm) fabric strip as shown, overlapping edges ¼" (6 mm) at center; zigzag to secure lapped edges. Cut strip in half.

7) Apply glue around middle of pen cap. Wrap fabric strip around cap, over glue; hand-stitch close to cap. Fold ends of strip to inside, forming spreader tab. Repeat for remaining pen cap.

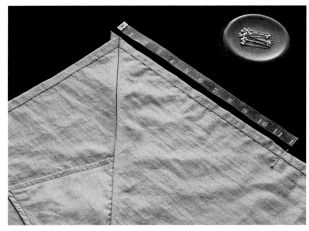

8) Mark points on each wing casing, 12" (30.5 cm) from nose tip, for placement of spreader tabs.

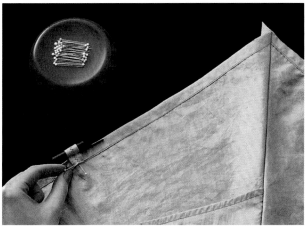

9) Pin the spreader tabs to the wings, with the tabs centered on marked points and with open ends of pen caps toward nose of kite. Stitch tabs to wings along stitching lines for casings.

10) Insert wing spars into wing casings. Insert spine in casing at center foldline. Stitch across casings at lower ends and nose tip.

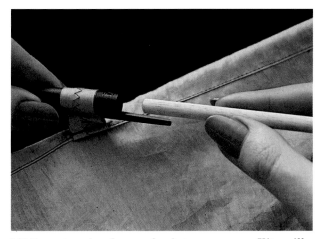

11) Insert ends of spreader into pen caps. Kite will hang loosely; spreader will not fall out.

12) Apply eyelet to tip of keel, following manufacturer's directions, just inside topstitching. Tie line securely to the keel.

How to Make the Pattern for an Arch-top Flexible Kite

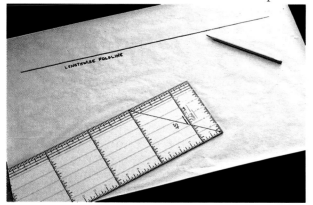

1) Draw 23½" (59.8 cm) line on paper, using pencil; label the line as the lengthwise foldline.

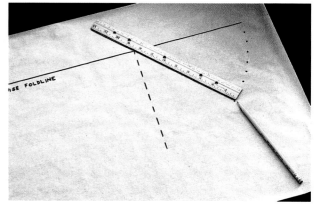

2) Mark a point on foldline, 8¼" (21.2 cm) from upper end. From this point, draw 8¼" (21.2 cm) dotted line, perpendicular to foldline. From same point, mark dotted line in 8¼" (21.2 cm) arc, using compass or straightedge, for upper portion of sail.

3) Draw 17½" (44.3 cm) dotted line, connecting end of 8¼" (21.2 cm) dotted line and the lower end of the foldline.

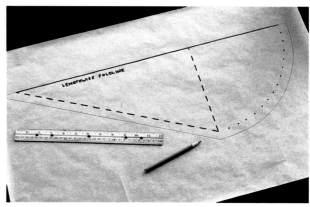

4) Draw cutting line, ¾" (2 cm) from dotted arc and straight line, for casing allowance.

How to Make an Arch-top Flexible Kite

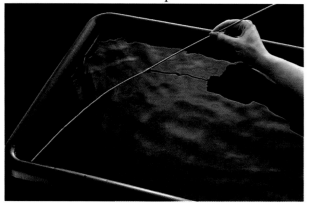

1) Place ⅛" (3 mm) dowel in warm water and allow to soak while following steps 2 to 4.

2) Fold the sail in half on foldline; press. Stitch ⅜" (1 cm) from foldline, to make casing for spine.

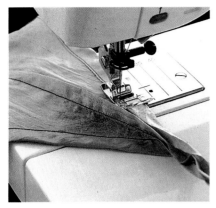

3) Hem the straight edges, turning under ¼" (6 mm), and then ½" (1.3 cm). Leave open at point, for inserting spine.

4) Make a casing on curved edge, pressing under ¼" (6 mm), then ½" (1.3 cm). Pin casing, placing pins close together. Stitch casing, stitching small pleats that form.

5) Remove dowel from water; wipe off. Bend dowel carefully, fastening one end to ironing board. Ease the dowel into the curved casing, while keeping dowel bent.

6) Cut ends of the dowel about 1" (2.5 cm) beyond the ends of the curved casing.

7) Insert the spine in center casing. Place two 5-ft. (1.58 m) tails at end of spine, one on each side, laying tails on sail. Secure tails, wrapping line tightly around end of spine. Turn tails down over end.

8) Fold 28" (71 cm) tail so that one end is 2" (5 cm) longer. Hand-stitch to gather tail at fold; secure to one end of curved dowel, taking several stitches into casing. Repeat for tail at opposite end of curved dowel.

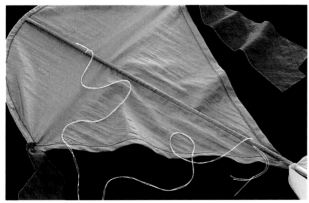

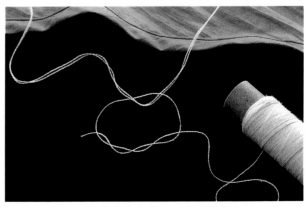

9) Mark points, 5½" (14 cm) and 19" (48.5 cm) from top of spine. Thread 96" (244 cm) line into needle. Stitch through kite, under spine, at points. Tie ends together securely next to spine, leaving 1" (2.5 cm) tails; this makes 47" (120 cm) double-strand bridle.

10) Attach line to bridle, tying a double overhand knot. The knot will self-adjust as the kite flies.

Teddy Bears

Although teddy bears can sometimes be time-consuming and difficult to make, this teddy with cut-on arms and legs is quick and easy to sew. Use the simplified pattern pieces on pages 84 and 85.

Select a wool flannel, textured wool, corduroy, velveteen, or robe velour. These fabrics are easier to work with than the usual fake fur and give a more old-fashioned quality to the bear. Hand-embroider the facial details to add to the old-fashioned appearance, or use the safety eyes and nose available at craft and fabric stores.

✄ Cutting Directions

Trace the partial pattern pieces (pages 84 and 85) and make full-size patterns as on page 82, step 1. Cut one back piece, placing the center back on a fold of the fabric. Cut two front pieces.

YOU WILL NEED

⅜ yd. (0.35 m) fabric, such as wool, corduroy, velveteen, or robe velour.

Embroidery floss.

Safety eyes and nose, optional.

Polyester fiberfill.

Pinking shears, optional.

Teddy bears can feature realistic safety eyes and nose or can be hand-embroidered for a more old-fashioned look.

How to Sew a Teddy Bear with an Embroidered Face

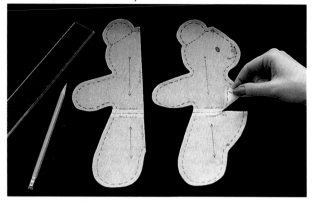

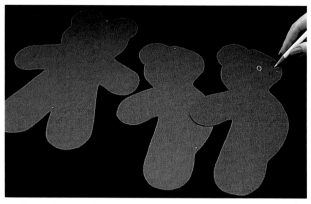

1) Trace partial patterns (pages 84 and 85) onto the tracing paper. Make full-size front pattern by taping front body and front leg pieces together, matching dotted lines. Make full-size back pattern, taping the back body and leg pieces together, matching dotted lines. Cut pieces from fabric as on page 81.

2) Transfer the dots at the top and bottom onto wrong sides of bear front and back pieces. Transfer pattern markings for eyes and dots at A, B, and C for nose and mouth, onto right side of bear front pieces.

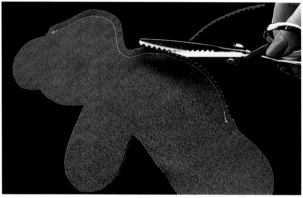

3) Stitch the center front seam from dot to dot. Notch curves with pinking shears, and clip inner corners with scissors. If pinking shears are not available, clip curves and corners with scissors.

4) Satin-stitch eyes at markings by stitching closely spaced parallel stitches, using three strands of embroidery floss.

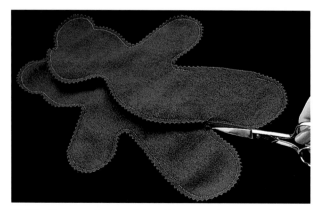

5) Pin front to back, right sides together, matching dots. Stitch around bear, leaving 3" (7.5 cm) opening on one side, along upper leg. Notch and clip the outer and inner curves as in step 3.

6) Turn the bear right side out. Stuff ears lightly with fiberfill. Using a zipper foot, stitch below the ears as indicated by dotted line on pattern.

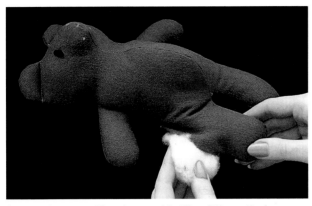

7) Continue stuffing bear with fiberfill until plump. Hand-stitch opening closed.

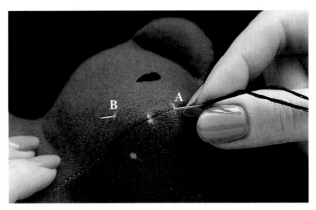

8) Thread needle with six strands of embroidery floss; knot ends together. Insert needle at Point A, bringing needle up at Point B on left side of mouth.

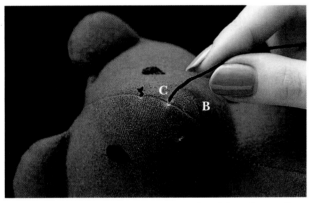

9) Insert needle at Point B on right side of mouth, bringing it up at Point C; to form curve of mouth, do not pull thread tight.

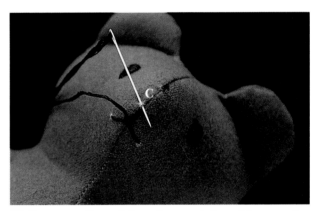

10) Loop needle and thread around thread for mouth; take small stitch at Point C, and do not cut threads. Satin-stitch nose vertically at shaded pattern area.

How to Sew a Teddy Bear with Safety Eyes and Nose

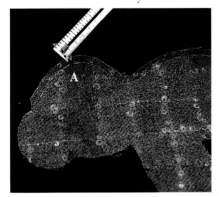

1) Follow steps 1 and 2, opposite. Stitch center front seam from dot at top of bear to Point A at the nose; secure stitching. Leaving ⅛" (3 mm) opening at nose, continue stitching seam to dot at bottom of bear; secure stitching.

2) Notch and clip center front seam allowances as in step 3, opposite. Stitch mouth as in steps 8 to 10, above; secure thread at Point C. Make small holes in bear front at markings for eyes, using awl. Insert shank of eye through hole.

3) Place locking washer over shank. Place bear face down on padded surface. Position thread spool over washer; tap gently in place, using hammer. Attach safety nose at the opening in center front seam. Finish bear as in steps 5 to 7, opposite.

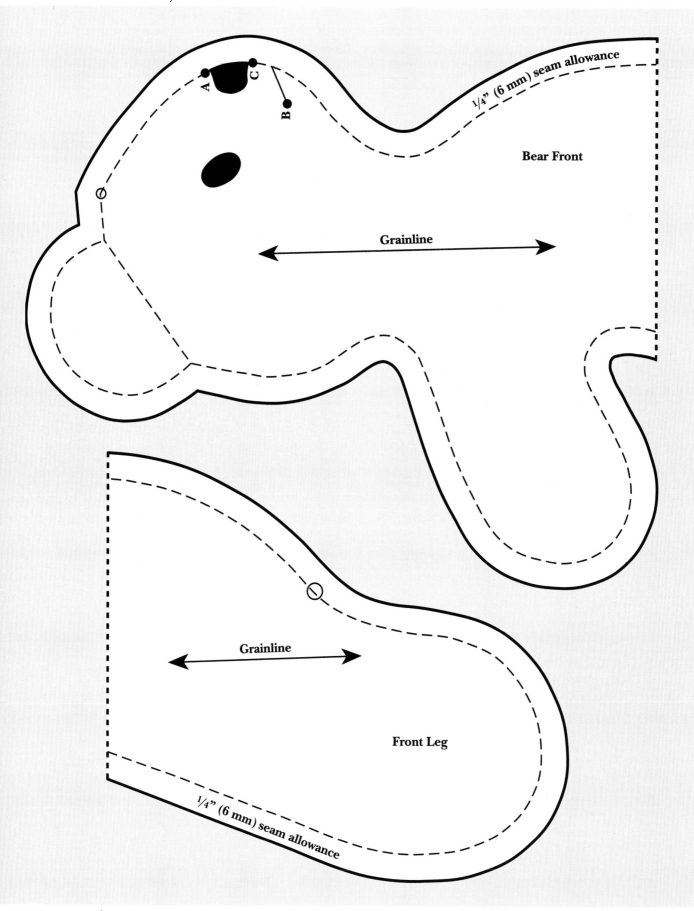

Bear Front

1/4" (6 mm) seam allowance

Grainline

Grainline

Front Leg

1/4" (6 mm) seam allowance

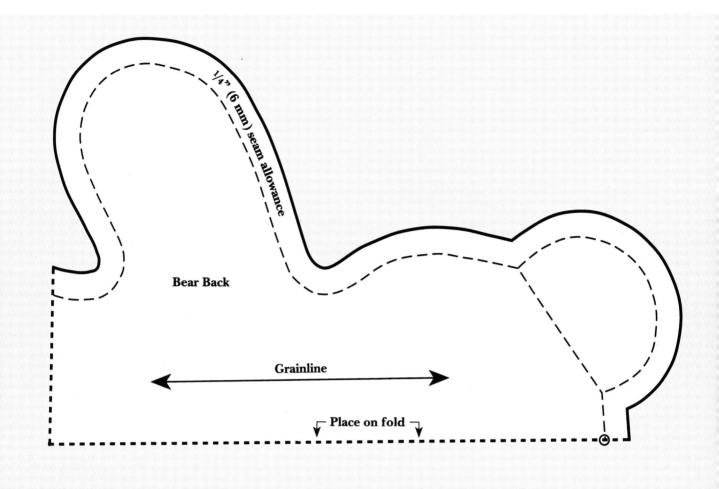

Bear Back

¼" (6 mm) seam allowance

Grainline

⌐ Place on fold ⌐

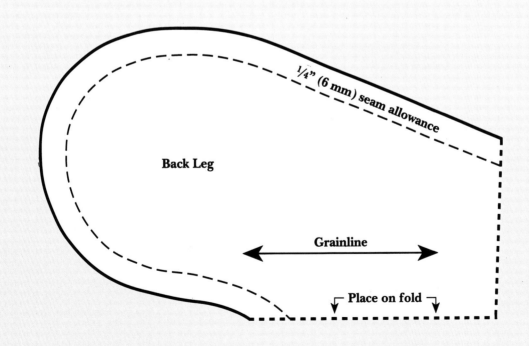

Back Leg

¼" (6 mm) seam allowance

Grainline

⌐ Place on fold ⌐

Hand Puppets

A ladybug and a daddy longlegs spider become hand puppets that are sure to delight any child. These crawling critters have gloves sized for a child's hand, allowing small fingers to become wiggly legs. Because both puppets have more legs than a child has fingers, the extra legs are stuffed to give them body. Made from two-way stretch fabric, such as swimwear fabric, these puppets can also be used comfortably by an adult.

✂ Cutting Directions

Prepare the puppet patterns, opposite. For each puppet, cut two bodies and two gloves from two-way stretch fabric; transfer the markings from the patterns. As in steps 4 and 5 on page 88, cut two eyes from felt or synthetic suede; for the ladybug puppet, also cut two wings from felt or synthetic suede, cutting out the dots on the wings.

YOU WILL NEED

½ yd. (0.5 m) two-way stretch fabric, for spider.

⅓ yd. (0.32 m) two-way stretch fabric, for ladybug.

Scraps of felt or synthetic suede, for eyes.

Scraps of felt or synthetic suede, for ladybug wings.

Polyester fiberfill, for stuffing.

Paper-backed fusible web.

How to Prepare the Hand Puppet Patterns

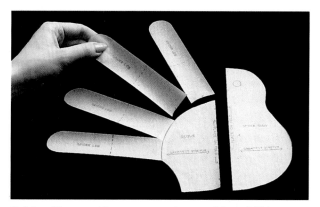

Ladybug. Trace ladybug patterns (pages 90 and 91) onto paper, tracing body, glove, and wing patterns once and tracing leg pattern three times. Tape three legs to curved edge of glove pattern.

Spider. Trace spider patterns (pages 90 and 91) onto paper, tracing body and glove patterns once and tracing leg pattern four times. Tape four legs to curved edge of glove pattern, overlapping legs slightly.

How to Sew a Ladybug Hand Puppet

1) Pin two glove pieces right sides together. Using short stitch length, stitch ¼" (6 mm) seam around legs; leave straight edge of glove unstitched. Clip seam allowances between legs.

2) Turn the glove right side out. Fold under ¼" (6 mm) on glove opening; stitch hem, using medium zigzag stitch.

3) Stuff one ladybug leg that will not be used for a finger when using the puppet.

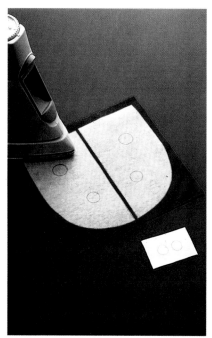

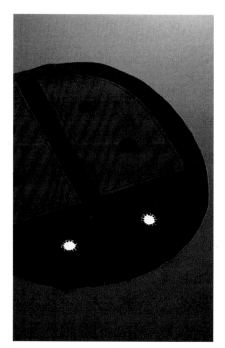

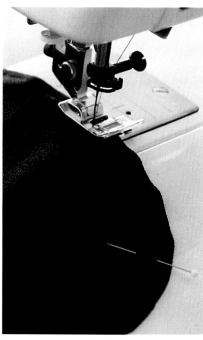

4) Trace eyes onto paper side of the paper-backed fusible web; cut. Fuse to the wrong side of synthetic suede or felt. Repeat for wings.

5) Cut out eyes and wings; fuse to upper body where indicated on pattern. Stitch around eyes, using short, narrow zigzag stitch. Stitch around wings, using straight stitch.

6) Cut 2" (5 cm) lengthwise slash in center of one body piece. Pin body pieces right sides together; stitch ¼" (6 mm) seam.

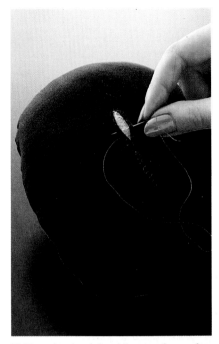

7) Turn body right side out through slash; stuff with fiberfill. Whipstitch slash closed.

8) Fold glove in half on foldline; position on underside of the body, matching markings, with foldline along the slashed line. Whipstitch glove to body along fold, taking care to catch only one layer of the glove in stitching.

9) Unfold glove; pin to the body at top of each leg. Slipstitch, using a double strand of thread; for the unstuffed legs, insert a finger into leg as you stitch, to catch only one layer of glove in stitching. For stuffed leg, catch both layers.

How to Sew a Spider Hand Puppet

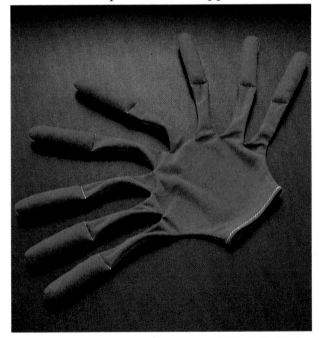

1) Follow steps 1 and 2, opposite. Stuff lower half of each spider leg with fiberfill; using zipper foot, machine-stitch across each leg at halfway point to form joint.

2) Stuff upper portion of three spider legs that will not be used for fingers. Complete the spider puppet, following steps 4 to 9, except omit wings.

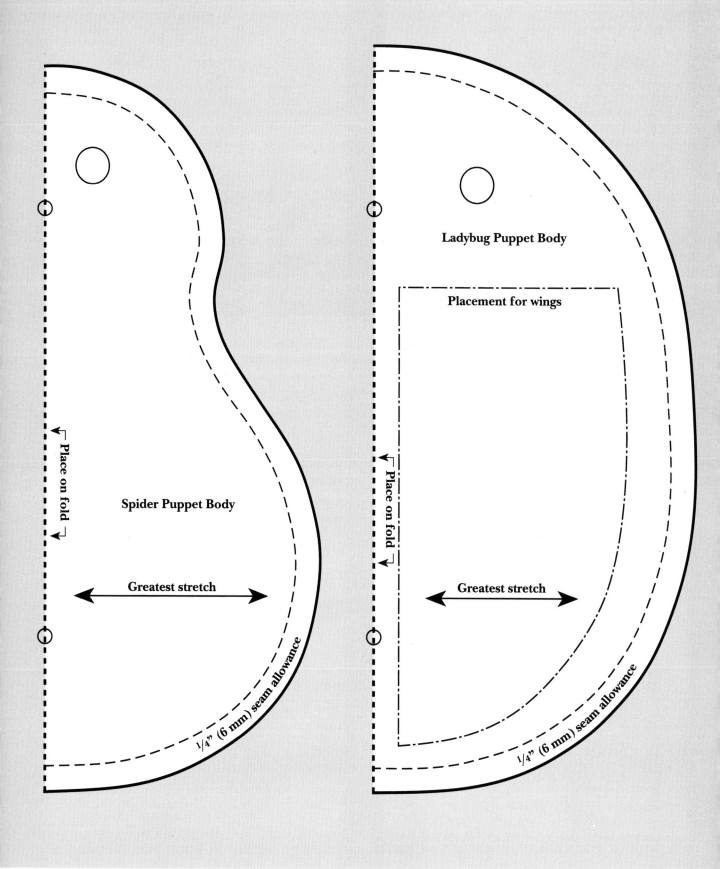

Ladybug Puppet Body

Placement for wings

Place on fold

Greatest stretch

¼" (6 mm) seam allowance

Place on fold

Spider Puppet Body

Greatest stretch

¼" (6 mm) seam allowance

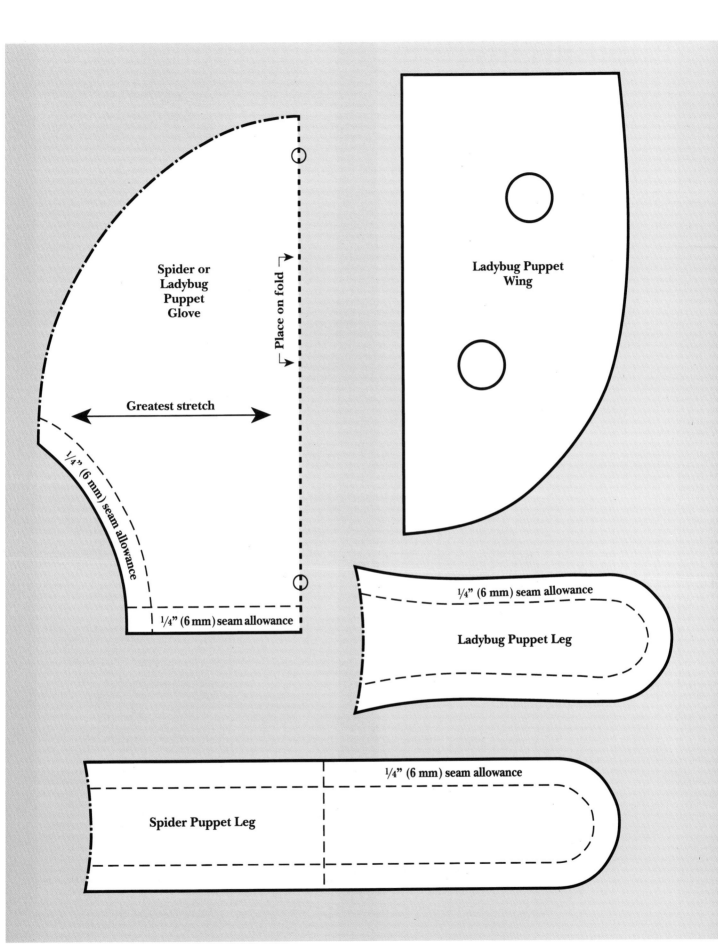

Spider or
Ladybug
Puppet
Glove

Place on fold

Greatest stretch

¹⁄₄" (6 mm) seam allowance

¹⁄₄" (6 mm) seam allowance

Ladybug Puppet
Wing

¹⁄₄" (6 mm) seam allowance

Ladybug Puppet Leg

¹⁄₄" (6 mm) seam allowance

Spider Puppet Leg

Playhouse Tents

This tent serves as either an indoor or outdoor playhouse. Supported by four ¾" (2 cm) PVC pipes, the tent can be erected quickly and easily by a child and stores compactly. The PVC pipe, available from hardware stores, is inexpensive, easy to cut, and very durable. A generous 54" (137 cm) on each side and 56" (142 cm) tall, the tent is large enough to share with friends.

For comfort, make the tent from cotton poplin or other mediumweight cotton fabric. Nylon fabric may also be used, but it will be hotter inside the tent. To add interest, select a bright-colored striped fabric for the casings.

✂ Cutting Directions

Cut three sides, one upper front, and two lower front sections, using the patterns on page 94, steps 1 to 3; for efficient use of the fabric, cut the pieces on the crosswise grain with the bottom of the pieces on the selvage. For the casings, cut 5" (12.5 cm) fabric strips on the crosswise grain; piece the strips together as necessary to make four 5" × 58" (12.5 × 147 cm) casing strips.

YOU WILL NEED

4½ yd. (4.15 m) fabric, 54" (137 cm) or wider, for the primary tent fabric.

⅞ yd. (0.8 m) fabric, 45" (115 cm) or wider, for the casing strips.

Four 68" (173 cm) lengths of ¾" (2 cm) PVC pipe.

Eight end caps for ¾" (2 cm) PVC pipe or for 1" (2.5 cm) chair legs.

One pair of shoelaces, 36" (91.5 cm) long.

Two squares of hook and loop tape.

Sandpaper.

Collapse the tent for easy storage, wrapping it like an umbrella and securing it at the bottom with the attached shoelace.

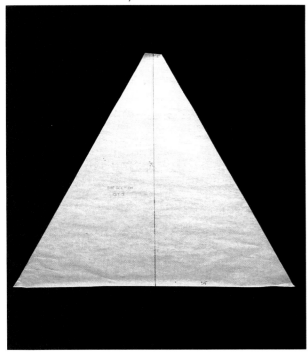

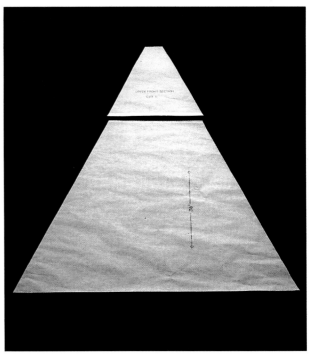

1) Draw 54" (137 cm) line for bottom of tent section. From center of this line, draw a perpendicular 54" (137 cm) line; draw 4" (10 cm) horizontal line, centered at end of this line. Connect ends of 4" (10 cm) line to ends of line at bottom. This trapezoid is the pattern for three sides of tent.

2) Draw a second trapezoid same size as in step 1; cut this trapezoid parallel to and 36" (91.5 cm) from bottom line. Add ½" (1.3 cm) seam allowance to edges where trapezoid was cut apart. Small trapezoid is pattern for upper front section.

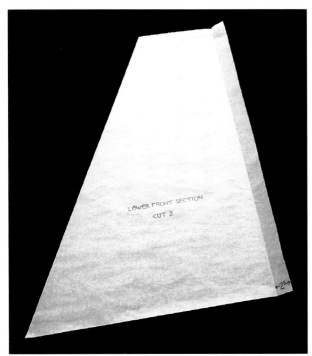

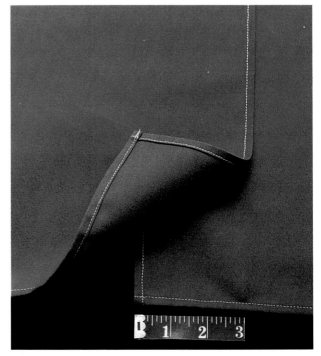

3) Fold bottom portion from step 2 in half lengthwise. Unfold, and draw a line, parallel to and 2" (5 cm) from fold; cut on line, and discard smaller piece. Larger piece is pattern for lower front sections. Cut fabric for tent (page 93).

4) Press under ¼" (6 mm) twice on vertical side of two lower fronts; stitch to make double-fold hems. Repeat for hems on lower edges. Overlap the two lower fronts 3" (7.5 cm); pin.

5) Align top edge of lapped lower front sections to bottom edge of upper front section, with pieces right sides together. Stitch ½" (1.3 cm) seam; finish the seam, using zigzag stitch.

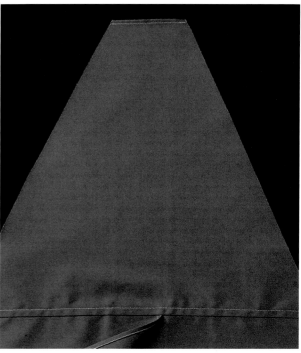

6) Press seam toward upper front section. Topstitch ⅜" (1.5 cm) from seam. Press and stitch ¼" (6 mm) double-fold hem on upper edge of front section.

7) Position squares of hook and loop tape at center of lower front opening (**a**) and near lower edge (**b**). Stitch in place.

8) Press and stitch ¼" (6 mm) double-fold hems on top and bottom edges of all remaining tent sections and on short ends of casing strips.

(Continued on next page)

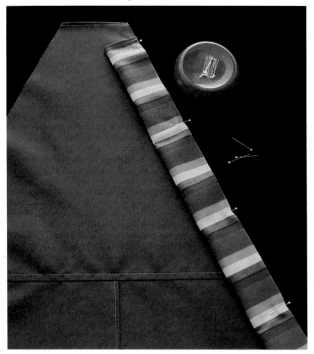

9) Fold a casing strip in half lengthwise, *wrong* sides together. Center folded casing strip on one diagonal edge of front section, with right sides together and raw edges even; pin.

10) Lay one side section of tent over the front section, right sides together, matching diagonal edges. Repin through all layers of tent and casing. Stitch ½" (1.3 cm) seam; finish seam, using zigzag stitch.

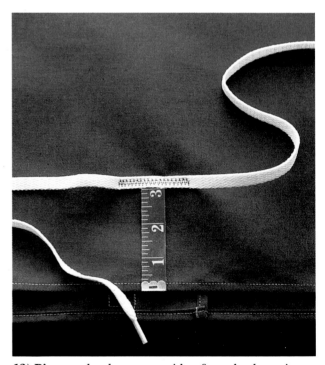

11) Apply remaining casings and stitch remaining diagonal seams of tent as in steps 9 and 10.

12) Pin one shoelace to outside of tent back section, centering it 3" (7.5 cm) from the lower edge. Stitch through the center of the shoelace for 2" (5 cm), using multizigzag stitch.

13) Drill hole completely through each PVC pipe, 4" (10 cm) from upper end, using ³⁄₁₆" drill bit.

14) Remove any labeling or other markings from the upper 15" (38 cm) of PVC pipes, using sandpaper.

15) Slide PVC pipes into casings, with holes at top of tent; apply end caps to top and bottom of each pipe.

16) Thread remaining shoelace through holes in the PVC pipes as shown. To erect tent, spread the pipes apart at bottom of tent and arrange them as shown on page 92.

Home Decorating Projects

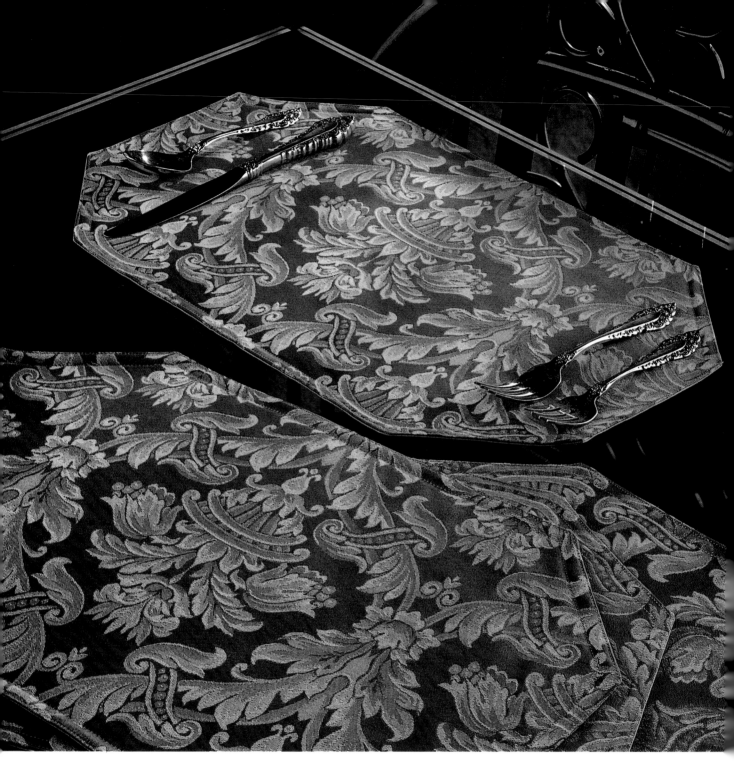

Octagonal Placemats

Because of their octagonal shape, these versatile placemats can be used equally well on a round or rectangular table. Made from contrasting decorator fabrics, the reversible placemats are lightly padded with polyester fleece. A set of four placemats can be made in an evening.

✂ Cutting Directions

For each placemat, using the pattern from step 1, cut one octagonal piece from each of the two fabrics,

with the short sides of the pieces on the lengthwise grain. Also cut one piece of polyester fleece for each placemat, using the pattern.

YOU WILL NEED

1 yd. (0.95 m) each of two fabrics, 45" (115 cm) wide, for four placemats.

1 yd. (0.95 m) polyester fleece, 45" (115 cm) wide.

How to Sew an Octagonal Placemat

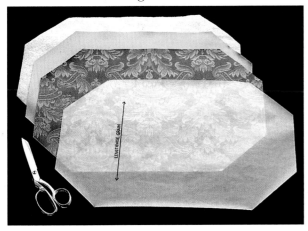

1) Draw 13" × 19" (33 × 48.5 cm) rectangle on paper. Mark points on each side, 3½" (9 cm) from corners; draw lines between marked points. Trim off corner areas, making pattern for placemat. Using pattern, cut fabrics and polyester fleece, opposite.

2) Press ½" (1.3 cm) seam allowance to wrong side on one short end of the placemat front and placemat back. Trim ½" (1.3 cm) from one short end of fleece.

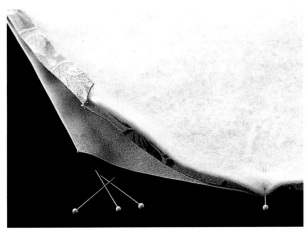

3) Place the placemat front and placemat back right sides together, matching edges and pressed ends. Place fleece on top, tucking trimmed end of fleece under folded seam allowance. Pin through all layers.

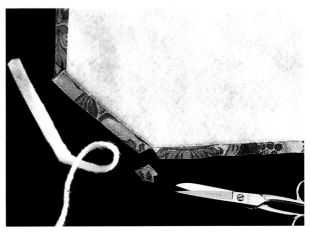

4) Stitch ½" (1.3 cm) seam around placemat, leaving pressed end unstitched. Trim fleece close to stitching. Notch seam allowances at corners, as shown.

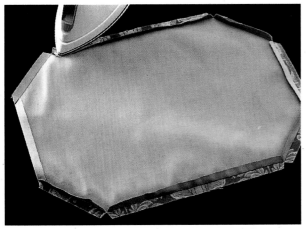

5) Lay placemat fleece side down. Press seam open. Turn placemat right side out; press edges.

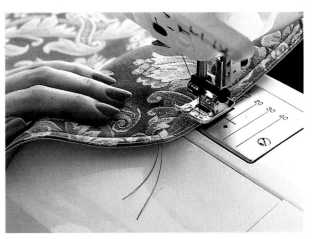

6) Pin opening closed. Topstitch around placemat, close to edges, and again ⅜" (1 cm) from edges.

Quilted Placemats & Table Runners

This placemat and table runner set is sewn using a machine-quilting method called "quilt-as-you-go." In this method, the batting is layered over the backing fabric, and the quilt pieces are sewn through the layers, piecing and quilting the project at the same time.

A single Square-in-a-Square Quilt Block is used for each placemat, with a border strip on each short end. The table runner consists of several quilt blocks, sewn in a row, with border strips at the ends of the runner and between the blocks.

The $11\frac{1}{2}$" (29.3 cm) quilt block, combined with two 3" (7.5 cm) border strips, makes a finished placemat that measures about $11\frac{1}{2}$" × $17\frac{1}{2}$" (29.3 × 44.3 cm). The table runner, made from four quilt blocks and five strips, measures about $11\frac{1}{2}$" × 61" (29.3 × 155 cm). To vary the length of the table runner, use a different number of quilt blocks or change the width of the strips at the ends and between the blocks.

Select five coordinating fabrics for piecing the quilt blocks. From the center out to the edges of the block, the fabrics are referred to as Fabric A through Fabric E. The yardage requirements at right are for either a set of four placemats or for one table runner.

Use a stitch length of 12 to 15 stitches per inch (2.5 cm). When piecing the fabrics together, it is not necessary to backstitch, because each seam will be intersected by another seam in the following step. Use an Even Feed® foot or walking foot, if available, to help prevent the layers from shifting as you sew.

✂ Cutting Directions (for one placemat)
From Fabric A, cut one $3\frac{3}{8}$" (8.5 cm) square for the center square of the placemat, and cut two $3\frac{1}{2}$" × 12" (9 × 30.5 cm) border strips.

From Fabric B, cut two $2\frac{7}{8}$" (7.2 cm) squares; cut the squares in half diagonally, to make four triangles.

From Fabric C, cut two $3\frac{3}{4}$" (9.5 cm) squares; cut the squares in half diagonally, to make four triangles.

From Fabric C, also cut two 2" (5 cm) strips across the full width of the fabric, to be used for the binding.

From Fabric D, cut two $4\frac{7}{8}$" (12.2 cm) squares; cut the squares in half diagonally, to make four triangles.

From Fabric E, cut two $6\frac{1}{2}$" (16.3 cm) squares; cut the squares in half diagonally, to make four triangles.

Cut one 14" × 20" (35.5 × 51 cm) rectangle each from backing fabric and batting.

✂ Cutting Directions (for one table runner)
For each quilt block in the table runner, cut fabric squares and triangles from Fabrics A through E, following the cutting directions for one placemat. From Fabric A, also cut five $3\frac{1}{2}$" × 12" (9 × 30.5 cm) border strips. From Fabric C, also cut four 2" (5 cm) strips across the full width of the fabric, to be used for the binding.

Cut one 14" × 20" (35.5 × 51 cm) rectangle each from backing fabric and batting. Cut three 14" × 17" (35.5 × 43 cm) rectangles each from backing fabric and batting. Cut the wide bias tape into three 12" (30.5 cm) lengths.

YOU WILL NEED

For four placemats or one table runner:
$\frac{1}{2}$ **yd. (0.5 m) Fabric A,** to be used for center of quilt block and for border strips.
$\frac{1}{4}$ **yd. (0.25 m) Fabric B.**
$\frac{1}{2}$ **yd. (0.5 m) Fabric C,** to be used for pieces of quilt block and for binding edges.
$\frac{1}{4}$ **yd. (0.25 m) Fabric D.**
$\frac{1}{2}$ **yd. (0.5 m) Fabric E.**
1 yd. (0.95 m) backing fabric.
Lightweight polyester quilt batt, in crib-quilt size, rinsed and machine dried.
1 yd. (0.95 m) wide bias tape to match backing fabric, for table runner only.

How to Sew a Quilted Placemat

1) Mark lines through center of the batting, in both directions, using lead pencil. Layer batting over backing, matching edges; pin in place.

2) Fold the center square of Fabric A in half, in both directions; finger-press center marks along each side. Place square flat at center of placemat, matching center of each side to marked lines on batting. Pin in place, with heads of pins toward center of square.

3) Place one triangle from Fabric B on the center square, right sides together, with diagonally cut side of triangle even with one side of square. At ends, allow points of triangle to extend equal distances beyond corners of square. Sew ¼" (6 mm) seam through all layers.

4) Turn the triangle right side up, finger-pressing along the seamline. Align point of triangle with marked line on batting; pin in place.

5) Repeat steps 3 and 4 for opposite side of square, then for remaining sides, using triangles from Fabric B.

6) Place ruler diagonally across center square; mark line on batting, using lead pencil. Repeat in opposite diagonal direction.

7) Apply set of triangles from Fabric C as in steps 3 to 5, aligning center of each triangle to marked line. Stitching lines should intersect the corners of center square exactly.

8) Continue in same manner for the set of triangles from Fabric D, then for triangles from Fabric E. Stitch one border strip to each side of placemat, aligning center of strip with corner of triangle in quilt block.

9) Smooth the border strips toward the outer edges of placemat. With a straightedge along edge of quilt block, trim excess fabric, batting, and backing, using rotary cutter. Or mark a line, and trim the layers with shears.

10) Press binding strips in half lengthwise, wrong sides together.

(Continued on next page)

11) Pin one folded binding strip to one long edge of the placemat top, matching raw edges, with end of strip extending 1" (2.5 cm) beyond end of the placemat. Stitch a scant ¼" (6 mm) from raw edges.

12) Wrap the binding strip snugly around edge of placemat, covering stitching line on back of placemat. From placemat top, pin in the ditch of the seam.

13) Stitch in the ditch on placemat top by stitching over the seamline in the well of the seam; catch the binding on the back of the placemat in the stitching.

14) Repeat steps 11 to 13 for opposite long edge of placemat. Trim ends of upper and lower binding strips even with edges of placemat.

15) Repeat step 11 for shorter ends of placemat. Trim ends of binding strips to extend ½" (1.3 cm) beyond finished edges of placemat.

16) Fold ½" (1.3 cm) end of the binding over finished edge; press in place. Wrap binding to back of placemat and stitch as in steps 12 and 13. Slipstitch ends.

How to Sew a Quilted Table Runner

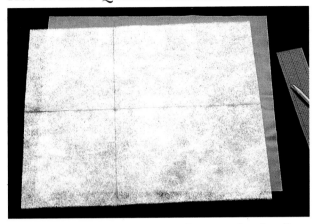

1) Mark 14" × 20" (35.5 × 51 cm) rectangle of quilt batting as on page 104, step 1; mark the three 14" × 17" (35.5 × 43 cm) rectangles of batting horizontally through center, and vertically 2" (5 cm) to one side of center. Layer batting pieces over backing pieces, matching the edges.

2) Stitch the quilt blocks as on pages 104 and 105, steps 2 to 9, stitching border strips to both short ends of the large rectangle and to one short end of the smaller rectangles.

3) Pin the large rectangle to one smaller rectangle along the end without the border strip, right sides together. Stitch ¼" (6 mm) seam through all layers.

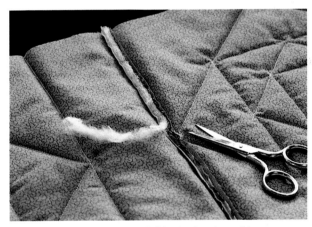

4) Join the remaining quilt blocks for the table runner as in step 3, left. Trim batting from seam allowances on back of the table runner.

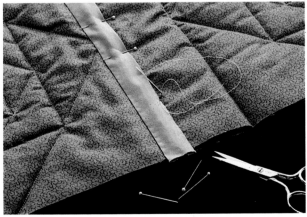

5) Pin one length of bias tape to back of the runner, centered over a seam; hand-stitch in place, catching backing fabric only. Repeat for all remaining seams. Trim ends of bias tape even with edges of runner.

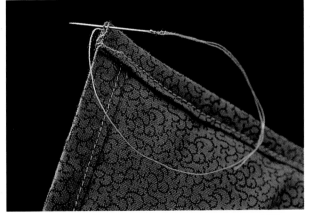

6) Apply binding to table runner as on pages 105 and 106, steps 10 to 16.

Easy Flange Pillows

A folded rectangle of fabric, sewn with flanged edges, may cover a pillow form for easy decorator pillows on sofas and chairs or be used as a sham for a bed pillow. The convenient overlap closure on the back is secured with hook and loop tape.

The center area of the pillow is equal to the size of the pillow form, but the flange size can vary. When deciding on the depth of the flanges, keep them in proportion to the pillow form. Flanges are often 2" to 3" (5 to 7.5 cm).

Flange pillow covers may be either unpadded or padded. Because of their simple design, they show off beautiful fabrics to the best advantage. They are often left unpadded for the easiest possible sewing.

For a Victorian look, make unpadded flange pillow covers with decorative overlays by adding an embroidered or lace-trimmed handkerchief, napkin, or placemat to the pillow front. For larger pillows, use large, dinner-size napkins with Venice, Cluny, or Battenberg lace borders. For smaller pillows, choose a delicate vintage hanky, such as those trimmed with cutwork or embroidery. The overlay on the front of the pillow extends into the flanges. The size of the pillow cover is based on the size of the overlay piece; for example, a dinner napkin 20" (51 cm) square can be used for a 16" (40.5 cm) pillow form and 2" (5 cm) flanges.

Padding the pillow cover with a thin layer of polyester quilt batting gives a softer look and adds body. For bed pillow shams, the padding also serves to prevent the pillowcase from showing through.

✄ Cutting Directions

Cut one rectangle from fabric, with the width of the rectangle on the crosswise grain. The width of the fabric rectangle is equal to the longest dimension of the pillow form plus twice the desired flange depth plus 1" (2.5 cm) for seam allowances. The length of the fabric rectangle is equal to two times the shortest dimension of the pillow form plus four times the desired flange depth plus 7" (18 cm) for the hems and overlap.

For a padded flange pillow, the batting and lining are cut as on page 111, step 1, after the pillow cover is stitched and turned.

YOU WILL NEED

Fabric, yardage depending on size of pillow.

Decorative handkerchief, napkin, or placemat for overlay on unpadded flange pillow cover.

Lining fabric, for padded flange pillow cover, slightly smaller than finished pillow cover including flanges.

Lightweight polyester quilt batting, for padded flange pillow cover, slightly smaller than finished pillow cover including flanges.

Square or rectangular pillow form.

2" (5 cm) length of hook and loop tape, ¾" (2 cm) wide.

How to Sew an Unpadded Flange Pillow

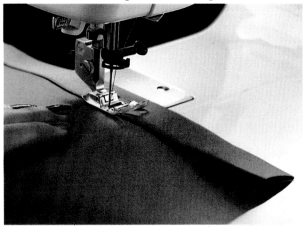

1) Press under 1" (2.5 cm) twice on both short ends of rectangle; stitch to make double-fold hems.

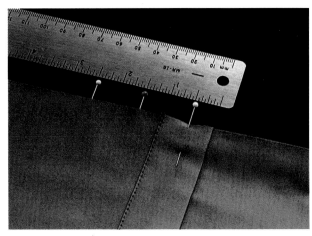

2) Mark center of each long edge. Fold fabric, right sides together, so the short ends overlap the center markings 1½" (3.8 cm) on each side. Pin in place along raw edges.

3) Stitch ½" (1.3 cm) seams. Clip corners diagonally. Turn pillow cover right side out; press.

4) Measure from edges of pillow cover to mark depth of flange on each side. Pin layers together. Stitch on marked lines, pivoting at corners, to form flange.

5) Pin hook side of hook and loop tape to overlap, centering tape on hem; stitch around tape. Pin loop side of hook and loop tape to the underlap, directly under hook side of tape; stitch.

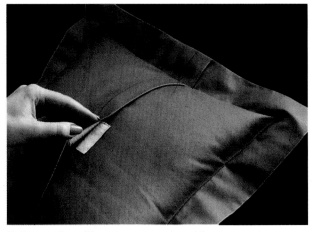

6) Insert the pillow form into the pillow cover. Secure the hook and loop tape.

How to Sew an Unpadded Flange Pillow with a Decorative Overlay

1) Follow steps 1 to 3, opposite. Center decorative napkin or handkerchief on pillow front; pin in place through all layers.

2) Measure from edges of pillow cover to mark the depth of the flange on each side of napkin. Stitch on the marked lines, pivoting at corners, to form flange. Complete pillow as in steps 5 and 6, opposite.

How to Sew a Padded Flange Pillow

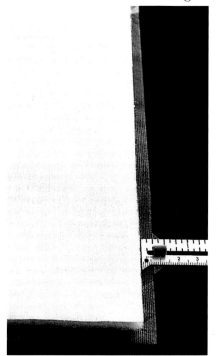

1) Follow steps 1 to 3, opposite. Cut batting and lining ¼" (6 mm) shorter than finished width and length of pillow cover, including the flanges.

2) Layer lining on top of batting. With lining side up, insert layers through opening in pillow cover; smooth in place.

3) Complete pillow as in steps 4 to 6, opposite. Use an Even Feed® foot or walking foot, if available, when stitching flanges; this helps prevent layers from shifting.

Trapunto Pillows

Create a pillow with a sculpted design, using the art of trapunto, a technique for stuffed quilting. In trapunto, the pillow front is backed with muslin and the entire design is outlined with hand stitching; then selected areas of the design are stuffed for a three-dimensional effect. Light plays off the design, creating highlights and shadows that make even a simple design look intricate.

For best results, use a smooth, solid-color fabric. The dimensional highlights and shadows are more striking if the fabric has a natural sheen, like satin or sateen.

Quilting patterns and stencil designs are often easily adapted for trapunto. Select a design with contained spaces that can be stuffed. In general, the best effect is achieved if you stuff the areas that would appear in the foreground of the design.

After the trapunto design is stitched on the pillow front, the pillow cover is constructed as a basic knife-edge pillow, with the front and back simply stitched together and turned right side out. The front and back are tapered toward the corners to prevent a dog-eared appearance on the finished pillow.

✂ Cutting Directions

From fabric, cut one pillow front and one pillow back, with the length and width 1" (2.5 cm) larger than the pillow form. Cut one piece each of the batting and muslin, to the same size as the pillow front.

YOU WILL NEED

Fabric, for pillow front and pillow back, yardage depending on size of pillow.

Muslin, for front lining.

Lightweight polyester quilt batting, yardage depending on size of pillow.

Polyester fiberfill.

Pillow form in desired size.

Water-soluble transfer paper.

Large embroidery hoop or quilting frame.

Crewel needle.

#5 or #8 pearl cotton.

How to Make a Trapunto Pillow

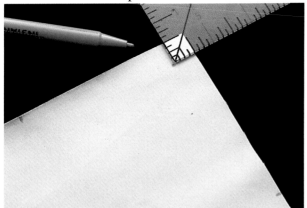

1) Fold pillow front into fourths. Mark a point halfway between corner and fold on each open side. At corner, mark a point ½" (1.3 cm) from each raw edge.

2) Mark lines, tapering from raw edges at center marks to mark at corner; cut on marked lines. Use pillow front as pattern for trimming the pillow back, muslin, and batting, tapering all corners.

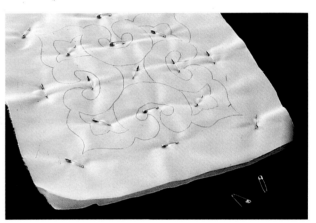

3) Center the trapunto design on the pillow front; transfer the design, using water-soluble transfer paper.

4) Layer muslin, batting, and pillow front. Pin-baste layers together with small safety pins, beginning at center and working toward edges.

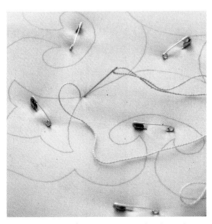

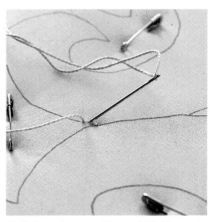

5) Place the pin-basted pillow front right side up in a large embroidery hoop or quilting frame. Thread a crewel needle with a single strand of pearl cotton thread, about 18" (46 cm) long; tie knot in end.

6) Backstitch trapunto design by bringing needle up to right side of pillow front, ⅛" (3 mm) from end of design line; pull thread through, and reinsert needle at end of the design line, to take first backstitch.

7) Bring the needle up ⅛" (3 mm) beyond the first stitch; pull thread through. Reinsert needle into the closest hole of first stitch. Continue to stitch in this manner to end of design line.

114

8) Knot the thread on the muslin side of the pillow front. Repeat for all design lines.

9) Decide which design areas are to be stuffed. For each area, cut small slit in muslin ½" (1.3 cm) to 1" (2.5 cm) long, depending on size of area.

10) Insert small amounts of fiberfill through the slits, stuffing the space between the muslin and batting to desired fullness. Use the eraser end of a pencil to help stuff any small areas.

11) Hand-stitch all slits in muslin closed. Pin pillow back to pillow front, right sides together. Stitch ½" (1.3 cm) seam, leaving opening on one side.

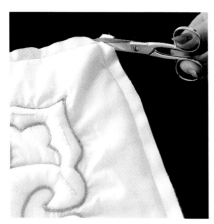

12) Trim corners diagonally, ⅛" (3 mm) from stitching. Turn the pillow cover right side out.

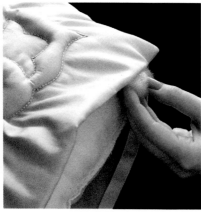

13) Press under seam allowances at opening. Insert pillow form. Stuff small amount of fiberfill into the corners, if desired, to fill them out.

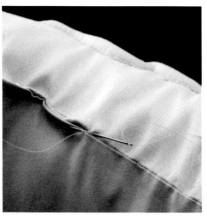

14) Pin opening closed. Slipstitch close to pressed edge, or machine edgestitch.

Gathered lamp shade cover with lace trim is made from lightweight cotton and accented with a small bow.

Lamp Shade Covers

Turn a small table lamp into a room accessory by adding a fabric lamp shade cover that coordinates with the room. For a romantic look, make a gathered shade cover, perhaps adding a lace trim. For a tailored effect, make a double-square shade cover. Both are suitable for 7" to 8" (18 to 20.5 cm) lamp shades.

For easy sewing, the gathered lamp shade cover has an elasticized casing. This eliminates the need to sew time-consuming ruffles and allows the lamp shade

cover to be easily fitted to the shade. The lower edge can be either hemmed or trimmed with lace. The double-square lamp shade cover is made from sheer or lightweight fabric, hemmed on all sides; the layers can be two different colors.

You may want to drape the fabric over the shade and turn on the light, to see whether the fabric color is affected. Lightweight fabrics allow more light to filter through.

✂ Cutting Directions

For a gathered lamp shade cover without lace trim, cut one fabric rectangle, 45" (115 cm) wide by the height of the lamp shade plus 5" (12.5 cm). The lamp shade cover will extend beyond the lower edge of the shade about 5/8" (1.5 cm). Cut 1/4" (6 mm) elastic equal to the distance around the top opening of the lamp shade plus 1/2" (1.3 cm).

For a gathered lamp shade cover with lace trim, cut one fabric rectangle, 45" (115 cm) wide by the height of the lamp shade plus the width of the lace trim plus 3 1/8" (7.8 cm). The lace trim will extend beyond the lower edge of the shade. Cut 1/4" (6 mm) elastic equal to the distance around the top opening of the lamp shade plus 1/2" (1.3 cm).

For the double-square lamp shade cover, cut two fabric squares equal to the measurement determined on page 119, step 1.

YOU WILL NEED

For a gathered lamp shade cover:

Small table lamp with 7" to 8" (18 to 20.5 cm) shade.

1/3 to 1/2 yd. (0.32 to 0.5 m) fabric, at least 45" (115 cm) wide, yardage depending on the size of the lamp shade.

3/8" (1 cm) strip of fusible web.

1/4" (6 mm) elastic, length equal to distance around top opening of lamp shade plus 1/2" (1.3 cm).

45" (115 cm) lace trim, optional.

1/4 yd. (0.25 m) ribbon, for optional bow.

For a double-square lamp shade cover:

Small table lamp with 7" to 8" (18 to 20.5 cm) shade.

3/4 yd. (0.7 m) sheer or lightweight fabric, 60" (152.5 cm) wide, if the same color is used for both layers. Or 3/4 yd. (0.7 m) each of two 45" (115 cm) fabrics, if different colors are used.

Gathered lamp shade cover is made from a chintz print to coordinate with a bedspread and curtains.

Double-square lamp shade cover has a tailored look. Shown here on a candlestick lamp, the shade cover is made from lightweight fabrics in two different colors.

How to Sew a Gathered Lamp Shade Cover

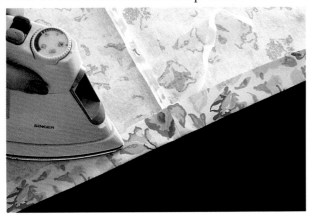

Shade with lower hem. 1) Stitch short ends of fabric rectangle together in ¼" (6 mm) seam; press open. Fold under 1¼" (3.2 cm) on lower edge; fuse hem in place, using a strip of fusible web, following the manufacturer's directions.

2) Fold under 1⅞" (4.7 cm) on upper edge; press. If fabric ravels easily, finish the raw edge, using zigzag or overlock stitch.

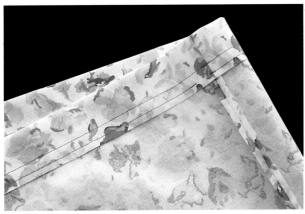

3) Stitch casing at upper edge by stitching two rows, 1¼" (3.2 cm) and 1⅝" (4 cm) from fold; leave small opening in the lower row of stitching, for inserting the elastic.

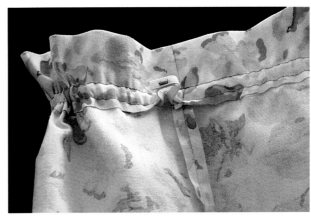

4) Insert elastic into casing. Overlap ends of elastic ½" (1.3 cm); stitch ends together. Place lamp shade cover on lamp shade. Hand-stitch a small ribbon bow to casing on front of lamp shade cover, if desired.

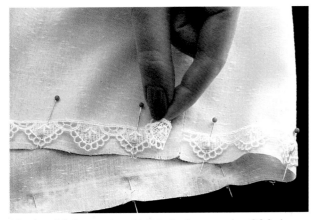

Shade with lace trim. 1) Stitch short ends of fabric rectangle together in ¼" (6 mm) seam; press open. Pin lace trim to fabric rectangle, right sides up, matching lower edge of lace trim to lower edge of fabric; overlap ends of lace ⅜" (1 cm) at seam.

2) Stitch along the upper edge of lace, using narrow zigzag stitch. From wrong side, trim fabric close to stitching. Zigzag through overlapped ends of lace; trim excess lace close to stitching. Complete the lamp shade cover as in steps 2 to 4, above.

How to Sew a Double-square Lamp Shade Cover

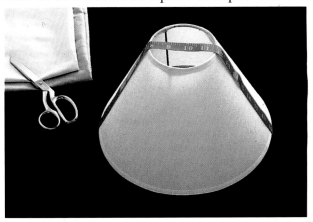

1) Measure the lamp shade from one side, over the top to the opposite side; add 2½" (6.5 cm) to this measurement for hem allowances. Cut two fabric squares to this size.

2) Press under ¼" (6 mm), then 1" (2.5 cm), on all sides of fabric squares. Stitch hem from edge to edge on each side, leaving long thread tails. Thread the tails into a needle, and conceal them between folds of fabric; trim excess thread.

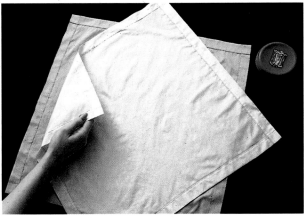

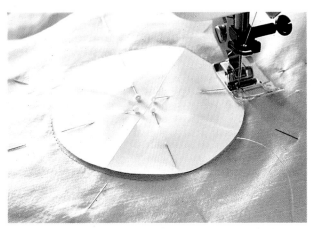

3) Fold the fabric squares into fourths; mark centers. Place upper fabric square on lower square, right sides down, matching centers; position them so corners of one square are evenly spaced between corners of the other. Pin layers together, using several pins.

4) Cut circle from paper, with the diameter of paper circle ½" (1.3 cm) smaller than the diameter of top opening of lamp shade. Fold paper circle in fourths to mark center; place on fabric squares, matching centers, and pin in place. Stitch around paper circle.

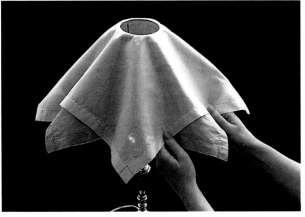

5) Remove the paper circle; trim away center of lamp shade cover to a scant ¼" (6 mm) from stitching, and clip seam allowances.

6) Turn lamp shade cover right side out; press. Place lamp shade cover over lamp shade; adjust points so they fall evenly.

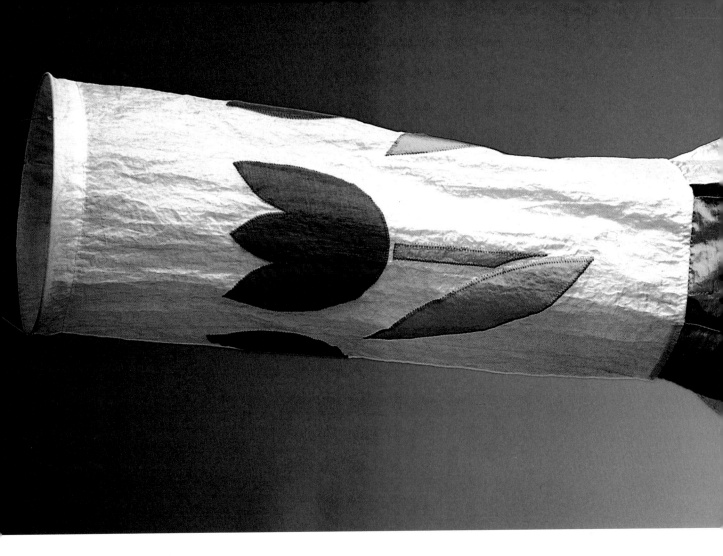

Wind Socks

A brightly colored wind sock is a cheerful accent for the yard or deck. Make one to be used year-round, or make several, embellishing each with seasonal appliqués. Draw simple appliqué designs like those shown here, or enlarge designs from coloring books or gift-wrapping paper to use as appliqué patterns.

Made from nylon fabric, a wind sock can withstand sunlight, rain, and other weather conditions without fading or deteriorating. Lightweight nylons, such as crinkled nylon, ripstop, and nylon broadcloth, are easy to sew and come in a variety of bright colors. Hung with sturdy nylon cording or fishline attached to a swivel, the wind sock can turn freely in the wind without tangling.

The instructions that follow are for a two-color or three-color wind sock with a total of six tails; the finished wind sock is about 38" (96.5 cm) long and 6" (15 cm) in diameter. You will need ½ yd. (0.5 m) of the fabric that will be used for the body of the wind sock; this allows enough fabric for two or three tails from the same color. You will need ¼ yd. (0.25 m) of the remaining color or colors, allowing enough for appliqués and two or three tails.

✄ Cutting Directions

Cut one 16½" × 18½" (41.8 × 47.3 cm) rectangle from the ½ yd. (0.5 m) piece of fabric, for the body of the wind sock. Cut a total of six tails on the crosswise grain of the fabric, each 3¼" × 22" (8.2 × 56 cm), cutting two or three tails from each color of fabric as desired.

As on page 122, steps 1 and 2, cut appliqués in the desired shapes and colors, from the remaining fabric.

YOU WILL NEED

½ yd. (0.5 m) fabric, for body of wind sock and tails.

¼ yd. (0.25 m) fabric in one or two colors, for appliqués and tails.

Paper-backed fusible web.

20" (51 cm) length of heavy rustproof wire.

Vinyl waterproof tape.

1 yd. (0.95 m) nylon cording or monofilament nylon fishline, for hanging the wind sock.

#5 or #6 ball-bearing swivel for fishing, to be used as the hanger.

Seasonal wind socks can be embellished with simple appliqué shapes, often found in coloring books.

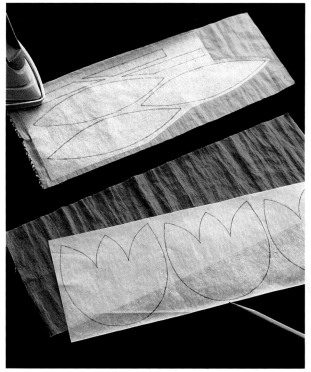

1) Trace desired appliqué shapes onto paper side of the fusible web; for asymmetrical designs, trace the mirror image. Apply the fusible web to wrong side of fabric, following the manufacturer's directions.

2) Cut the appliqué pieces, following marked lines on the fusible web; remove the paper backing.

3) Arrange appliqué pieces on the body of the wind sock, allowing for ¼" (6 mm) seams at the side and lower edges and 1" (2.5 cm) casing at the top. Fuse appliqués in place.

4) Stitch around appliqués with short zigzag stitches of medium width.

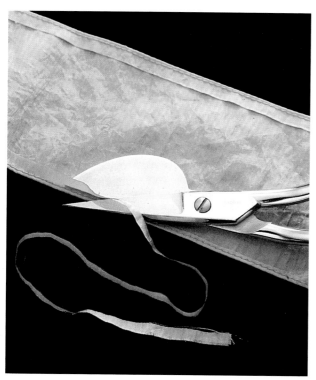

5) Turn long edges of tails ¼" (6 mm) to wrong side; stitch close to fold. Trim the excess fabric close to the stitching.

6) Turn long edges to wrong side again, enclosing raw edges. Stitch over the previous stitches.

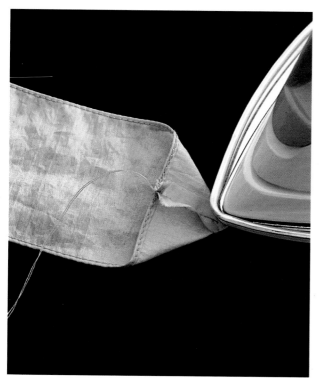

7) Fold lower end of tail in half, right sides together. Stitch ¼" (6 mm) seam across end. Press seam open.

8) Turn end of tail right side out, to form point; press. Stitch and turn remaining tail ends.

(Continued on next page)

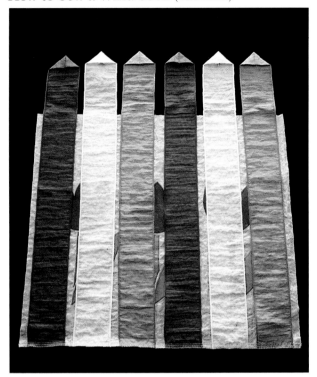

9) Pin tails along lower edge of body, with right sides together and raw edges even; leave ¼" (6 mm) seam allowance on sides of body. Stitch ¼" (6 mm) seam on lower edge; finish seam, using overlock or zigzag stitch.

10) Turn seam toward wind sock body, with the tails extending down. Topstitch seam in place.

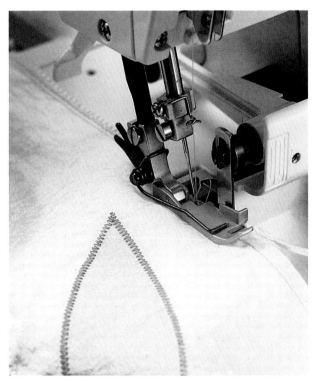

11) Fold wind sock body in half, matching raw edges at side; stitch ¼" (6 mm) seam. Overlock or zigzag seam allowances together. Turn the wind sock right side out.

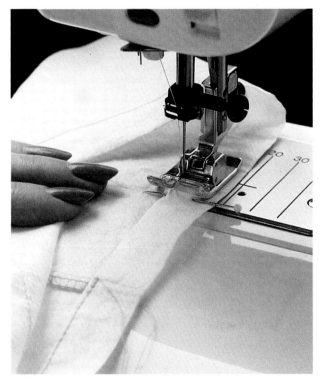

12) Press under ¼" (6 mm) on the upper edge of the wind sock. Then press under ¾" (2 cm); pin in place, to form casing. Stitch close to the first fold, leaving 2" (5 cm) opening for inserting wire.

13) Insert 19" (48.5 cm) length of wire into casing. Wrap the overlapped ends of wire together with waterproof tape. Stitch opening in casing closed.

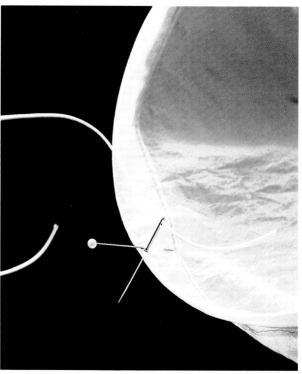

14) Divide top of wind sock into thirds; mark. At each mark, take a single stitch through casing, just below the wire, using large-eyed needle and 12" (30.5 cm) length of nylon cording or fishline.

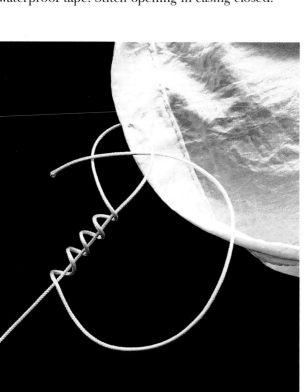

15) Tie end of nylon cording or fishline securely to wind sock as shown.

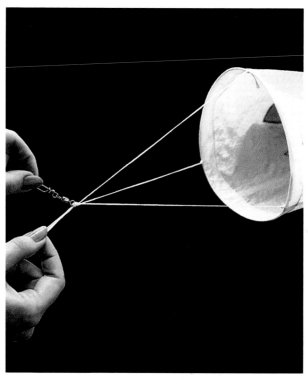

16) Hold ends of cords together, keeping the lengths equal. Thread ends through the eye of ball-bearing swivel; tie securely. Hang wind sock.

Index

Cy DeCosse Incorporated offers
a variety of how-to books. For
information write:
    Cy DeCosse Subscriber Books
    5900 Green Oak Drive
    Minnetonka, MN 55343